THE MONTANA STRANGLERS

IN DAKOTA TERRITORY

RON N. BERGET

THE History PRESS

Published by The History Press
Charleston, SC
www.historypress.com

Front cover, top: Rufus Zogbaum sketch of the Montana Stranglers at James wood yard. *Yale Collection of Western Americana, Beinecke Rare Book and Manuscript Library, Yale University*; *background*: Rice's Sectional Map of Dakota Territory, 1876. *Library of Congress*; *bottom*: *Men of the Open Range*. Charles M. Russell, oil on canvas, 1923. *Montana Historical Society Mackay Collection, X1952.01.09*. This is how the Stranglers would have looked riding out of the Missouri River valley in Dakota Territory. Flopping Bill rode a white horse named Snowball just like the leader in this painting. *Back cover, top*: The Weller stage stop, McLean County, DT. *Date: 1883 1889. Collection: 10158 Folder: 0003.000 Item: 00026 SHSND*; *inset*: Flopping Bill, stock detective. Sketch based on a photo in *Kaleidoscope Lives* by Joseph Taylor. *Sketch by Sarah Johannsen*; *bottom*: A Bad Lands cowboy, 1887. *Charles Bregler's Thomas Eakins Collection, purchased with the partial support of the Pew Memorial Trust. 1985.68.2.1076 Pennsylvania Academy of Fine Arts.*

First published 2022

Manufactured in the United States

ISBN 9781467149716

Library of Congress Control Number: 2022939459

Notice: The information in this book is true and complete to the best of our knowledge. It is offered without guarantee on the part of the author or The History Press. The author and The History Press disclaim all liability in connection with the use of this book.

CONTENTS

There is a way which seems right to a person, but its end is the way of death.
—Proverbs 14:12

This story does not have many good guys.

ACKNOWLEDGEMENTS

My father, on whose farm I was free to ride, shoot, hunt and fish. Many is the time I heard him cuss that damn wind. He told me a tale about Hangman's Point when I was a boy many decades ago. I was driven to find the whole truth—this book is the result.

Thanks to the many historical preservation organizations, especially the North Dakota State Historical Society and the groups from McLean, McHenry, Mercer and Ward Counties of North Dakota.

A special thanks to Doug Ellison at Western Edge Books in Medora. He generously shared his notes on this topic. You must thank him for many of the details related to the Bad Lands part of this story.

Thanks to Karen and the rest of my family who encouraged me, listened patiently to me as I droned on about "my book" and helped in many ways.

THREE CENTRAL CHARACTERS:

Red River Métis
Francis Gardipee,
alleged horse thief.

Ex–Bismarck mayor
Edmund Hackett,
crony capitalist.

Stock detective
Flopping Bill Cantrell.

Sketches by Sarah Johannsen.

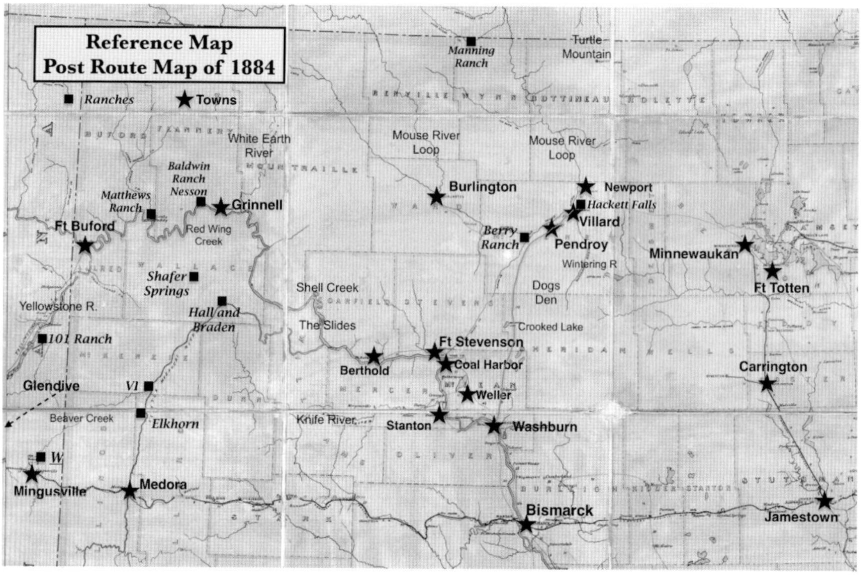

Reference map created with the Post Route Map 1884. *W.L. Nicholson United States Post Office, found in the David Rumsey Map Collection, David Rumsey Map Center, Stanford Libraries.*

INTRODUCTION

It is May 1886. Henry Tuncil and William McKay arrive at a point of land jutting out into the middle of Crooked Lake, Dakota Territory. They have come looking for jumbo yellow perch. A northwest wind tips the waves with a white froth, so the Washburn fishermen move to the leeward side of the point and wade waist deep to get past the brown, broken pencil reeds. The cold water numbs their legs.

Long poles swing lines with a float, a hook and a weight set down about three feet. "*Another snag*," Tuncil cusses under his breath. He gives it a productive tug, then a harder pull. A large object succumbs and rises to the surface. It rolls over before his eyes—he is looking into a human face. It is drawn in a grisly smile, disfigured, mouth agape in a silent beg for justice.

The story you are reading is true.[1] The face has a name: Francis Gardipee. He is not alone. Two others are with him in the chilled waters. Stanley Ravenwood is the name of one; John Bates is the name of the other. A vigilante group called the Montana Stranglers murdered Gardipee in November 1884. He and the others were clubbed and shot, their bodies bound with lariats, then stuffed into the icy grave to hide the shame. To those who live here today, they know this place as Hangman's Point. Local people are aware of the name, but few know the tale it longs to tell. Even fewer have ever heard the names of these murdered or the over fifty others killed just like them. The only justice for them now is for us to hear and remember their story.

THE OUTLAWS

In March 1882, a Prussian immigrant, Charley Rhodes (aka Dutch Charley), was playing cards and losing badly in Coulson, Montana. Charley was angrily complaining when an eighteen-year-old waiter innocently asked, "What's the matter with you?" The irritated Rhodes punched the unarmed teen in the face, and the boy fell to his knees. Dutch Charley then shot the young man through the neck and heart. While on the run, a couple of months later, he killed another man named Mitchell north of Miles City. Dutch Charley had a deep criminal past—killing at least seven if we can believe the newspapers.[2]

With lawmen pursuing him, he hid out in the wild Missouri River breaks at the mouth of the Musselshell River.[3] Here he connected with horse thieves who were preying on the new ranches around Maiden and elsewhere in central Montana. They took the stolen stock to their camps and then relayed them into Canada or along the Missouri River into Dakota Territory.

From this pool of Musselshell derelicts, Dutch Charley organized his own gang of thieves in the spring of 1883. He found willing recruits in Stanley Ravenwood and John Bates, who were later found on the bottom of Crooked Lake. Also in the gang were Bill Smith and Dutch Charley's bookkeeper, James Rutherford. Dutch Charley and his small gang collected a herd of stolen Montana horses. Following the Missouri River, they drove them east into Dakota Territory (DT). They brought the horses through a new settlement on the Mouse River called Burlington. Two members of the gang, Ravenwood and Bates, made this their home.

Dutch Charley, Smith and Rutherford moved on from Burlington and set up a camp within half a mile of the Canada border west of Turtle Mountain. This became the last relay station. Horses stolen from the fresh new communities to the south were likely brought here in this unsettled borderland and then slipped into Canada for sale.

The Great Northern Railroad was working its way toward Burlington, Dakota Territory. Ravenwood and Bates claimed to be railroad contractors ready to sell horses to the builders when they arrived. It should have been a red flag that the herd was a mix of many Montana brands, but most of the people in the town trusted and accepted them.

There were other outlaws in Dakota engaged in the same enterprise. These groups probably worked together, at least in part. Jim Smith had a camp on the White Earth River. Some Métis (May-tee, French for "mixed") operated out of Turtle Mountain. Métis near the village of Villard at the confluence of Wintering and Mouse River were also getting into the action. This was the home of Francis Gardipee, the third man found in Crooked Lake.

THE VIGILANTES

In the summer of 1884, Stuart's Montana Stranglers murdered twenty alleged horse thieves in Montana Territory. This event became an archetype from which writers have drawn novels and movie scripts.[4] Historians and authors have documented the Montana part of the story well. What is not as well known is that the work of the Stranglers continued in the fall of 1884 into Dakota Territory until the killing ended in the lakes and buttes country near Dogden Butte and along the Missouri River in McLean County, DT. From the fall of 1883 to December 1884, there were other killings by other vigilantes and horse thieves—fifty-four between the combined groups, maybe more.

HANGED WITHOUT LAW

The depredations of the outlaws on the recently established farms and ranches in Dakota and Montana created an unbearable hardship. Frustration boiled over into violent action. Official law enforcement was thinly stretched over vast distances, so local communities formed their own vigilance committees or regulators to protect themselves from these horse thieves, claim jumpers and prairie fires. This, combined with a "lynch first and ask questions later" mindset, created a deadly environment.

The same scenario unfolded in much of the West in the 1880s. *The Post*, out of Billings, Montana, published the following report from southern Montana, August 1883:

> *Since January—65 hanged by law, 71 hanged without law, 22 were negroes.*[5]

This book tells the story of how a similar deadly environment played out in Dakota Territory in 1883–84. The same activities in north-central Montana in the summer of 1884 are connected, so the two are combined. This book documents the deaths of fifty-four in the Upper Missouri River and Mouse River country, most murdered "*without law*."

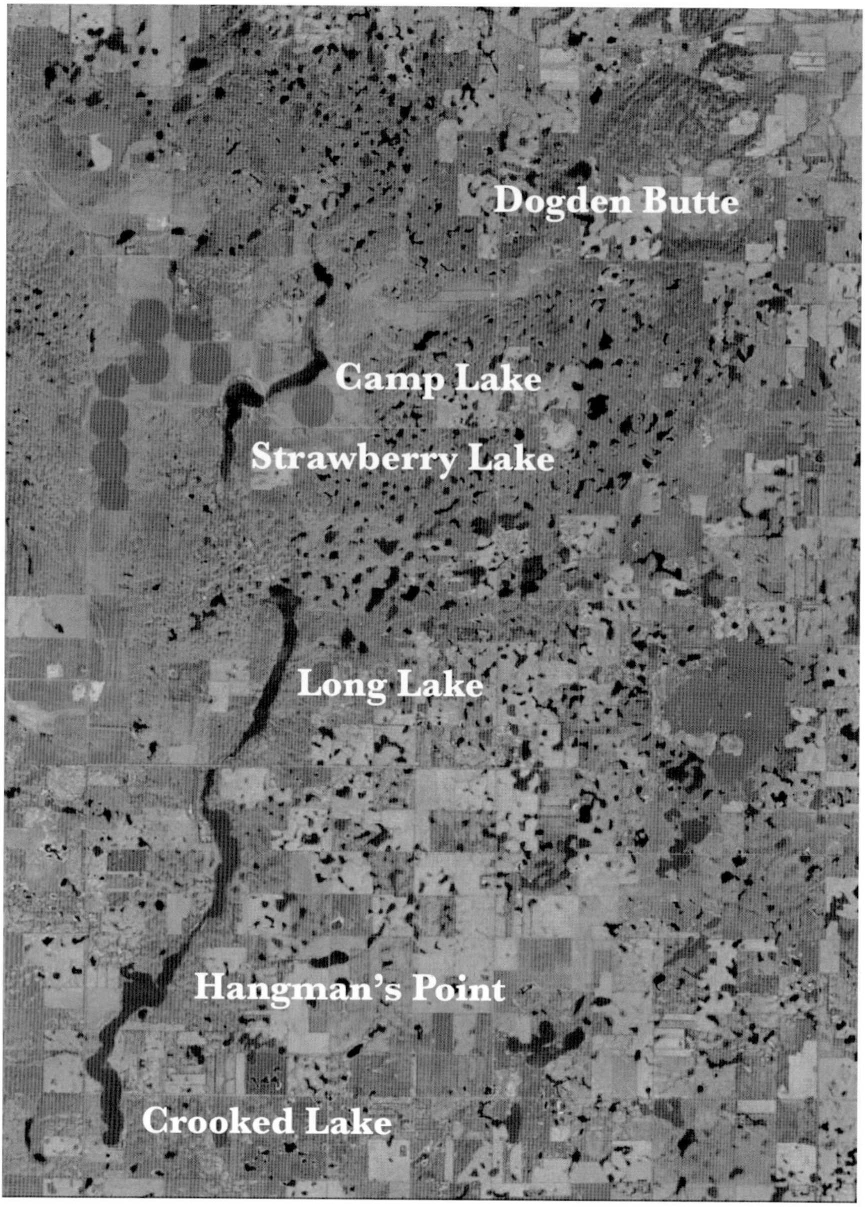

Above: Dogden Butte and Strawberry Lake Chain, McLean County, North Dakota. *Google Earth Pro*.

Opposite: Hangman's Point at Crooked Lake. *Photo by Eric Berget*.

Each of the fifty-four killed represents a human life story. The choices people make for good or ill create history. These choices become role models or cautionary tales for the generations to follow. Even today, we see people acting without law when law does not act.

GARDIPEE, HACKETT AND FLOPPING BILL

Three characters stand out in this story:

The first is Francis Gardipee, the alleged Métis horse thief. He is an everyman, caught in the web of cultural change.

Next is Edmund Hackett, the Yankee crony capitalist driven to succeed no matter the cost to others.

The third is Flopping Bill Cantrell, leader of the Stranglers, who, given authority, abuses it for his convenience. He appoints himself judge, jury and executioner whenever it suits his needs.

The three together, and other surrounding characters, provide a historical snapshot of the people and events that were the true Old West as it occurred in northern Dakota Territory and Montana in 1883 and 1884.

1

FRANCIS GARDIPEE

Métis Mail Carrier Turned Horse Thief

Two men pack mail next to a fireplace framed by prairie boulders. George Hoffman was the first postmaster of Villard, and Francis Gardipee was a local "half-breed" he recruited to carry the mail.[6] They loaded precious Christmas greetings to families far away from this fledgling wilderness community. The door opened, and the prancing flames revealed the shadows of eager sled dogs, waiting in the morning cold.

Francis was a thin man with high shoulders and dark, piercing eyes. He loved to dance the jig, and a pipe was ever present in his mouth. Like most Red River Métis, he was full of life and fun. He was well-liked by the neighbors newly settled by his home, and he had welcomed them.[7]

In December 1883, the Villard, DT post office was a two-room log building with a sod roof and a dirt floor. The only way to get mail to and

Francis Gardipee. No photograph exists of Gardipee. This artist's depiction is based on pictures of Métis in 1883. *Sketch by Sarah Johannsen.*

The Pendroy Post Office. The Pendroy clan drove the first herd of cattle into the Mouse River country in 1883. Picture probably includes Johnny Pendroy, Tom and Belle Berry and Marion Pace—people mentioned in this book. *Collection: 00054 Folder: 0001.000 Item: 00004 State Historical Society of North Dakota (SHSND).*

from this remote location in the Mouse River Valley in winter was by dogsled from Washburn, DT, seventy-five miles to the south.

To Hoffman and the handful of American and Norwegian settlers in Villard, this was the advance of civilization deep into the Dakota wilderness. They viewed themselves as pioneers settling fresh territory. For Francis Gardipee, this was his backyard. Gardipee's log shack created a safe hamlet that was his family's home. It had been a Métis hivernant (overwinter hunting camp) for decades. The Red River Métis had hunted, trapped and traveled these trails in Central Dakota for one hundred years.

Hoffman first hired two Native Americans to carry the mail in the summer of 1883. They failed to return from Washburn. He searched south along the trail and found them in a drunken stupor at the midway station cabin. He fired them on the spot. They were deeply shamed and plotted his murder to regain honor. Lucky for Hoffman, when they arrived at his cabin to execute the plan, they encountered his wife first. She had always been kind to them, so for her sake they let it go.[8]

Hoffman turned to Francis Gardipee and entrusted him with the job for the fall and winter of 1883–84. Gardipee put into practice skills developed during years of winter buffalo hunting and as a mail carrier with the U.S.

military. It was likely this Gardipee who had worked at Fort Stevenson, DT, in the late 1860s as a scout and Pony Express rider. He braved many dangers from the Lakota and severe weather.[9] This experience, and his intimate knowledge of the area, made him more than qualified as a mail carrier for Villard.

THE ROAD TO THE MANDAN

Gardipee made this trip to sell furs at the trading posts on the Missouri River countless times. This was the Road to the Mandan Indians, a trail older than memory.

The mail loaded, Gardipee set off with a *Hike!* and a crack of the whip. His four-dog team gave a hard pull, and the eight-foot toboggan broke free into the crisp predawn moonlight. Gardipee and the dogs bolted out into the snow-bound prairie wilderness. He called *Gee!* for right and *Haw!* to the left. The ten-foot trail rope was in his hand as he jogged beside the dogs. On uphill runs, he used the rope as a tow to assist his climb but rode downhill on the back of the sled.[10] With wind-packed snow, they might complete this ultramarathon in one interminable day. Even the most skilled plainsman

Huskie Dogs on the Frozen Highway, by Frederic Remington. Remington did several sketches and paintings of the Red River Métis people. *Granger Historical Picture Archive.*

must respect the open prairie and the deadly wind of Dakota. Under certain conditions, the blowing snow whites out all landmarks over the barren hills. It is easy to lose your way in this wind.

The Road to the Mandan, as used during the fur trade era, started on the Assiniboine River at Brandon, Manitoba. It headed south along the west side of Turtle Mountain, crossed the Mouse River first at Willow Creek and then crossed again at the mouth of the Wintering River near Gardipee's log home. Gardipee jumped on this ancient path as it moved west along the Mouse River to gather the mail at Pendroy. From there, his journey paralleled the Wintering River, south to the base of the Grand Coteau, west of Maison Du Chien.

DOG DEN BUTTE AND THE GRAND COTEAU

The Grand Coteau is a plateau of steep rolling hills that follow a day's ride on the east side of the Missouri River. At this spot on the Grand Coteau is a prominent hill that the Mandan named Mashugadish. To the Sioux, it was Sunka Oti. Among the French-speaking Métis, it was Maison Du Chien. The Dogsden or Dogs House or Dogden Mountains or Dogden Butte are all the unique ways Americans translated this name.

At the first crack of morning light, Gardipee, thinking in the French patois (Michif) that was his native tongue, saw Maison Du Chien straight ahead. It is near here that the road to the Mandan intersects with the Totten Trail at Strawberry Lake. This turns west down into Horseshoe Valley. Totten Trail was the road used to supply Fort Totten on Devils Lake from Fort Stevenson on the Missouri. In August 1883, Fort Stevenson was closed, so all mail came from Washburn.

In times past, to trade on the Missouri and haul mail to and from Washburn, Gardipee followed the Road to the Mandan heading south at Dogden Butte. This trail follows a nine-mile-long chain of named lakes—Camp, Strawberry, Long, Crooked and an unnamed creek from Crooked Lake that drains the area south of the Butte.[11] If he followed this creek south, he would have come to the shallow lakes in what is now Lake Nettie National Wildlife Refuge. A butte to the east (the Wolf Hills) oriented his bearings south toward Turtle Lake, from which he would follow Turtle Creek to the Missouri.

1814 Map of Ossiniboia. Note faint line depicting the Road to the Mandan. Also note Dogshouse Hill prominently displayed. *SHSND OCLC262846054.*

FORTS, TOWNS AND CHANGE

The U.S. military built Fort Stevenson in the summer of 1867 for the gold miners who plied the Missouri River heading to Montana; these travelers needed forts to protect them from the Sioux. Fort Rice, Fort Buford and Fort Stevenson were built along the Missouri River. Fort Stevenson was the fort closest to Dogden Butte. They placed Fort Totten at Devils Lake, one hundred miles to the east.

Other frontier settlements sprang up along the Missouri River. They knew Gardipee well in Washburn. Like Villard, American pioneers had founded Washburn only a year and a half earlier in 1882 as a riverboat town upstream from Painted Creek. Painted Woods Lake lay downriver. South beyond Painted Woods was the railroad town of Bismarck, only one decade old.

As Gardipee passed Dogden Butte, childhood training and memories put him on high alert. When he was nine years old, two thousand Yanktonai Dakota attacked a group of seventy Métis buffalo hunters and their families at this very place. Miraculously, the Métis lost only one man. After a two-day siege, a larger hunting party containing Gardipee's family came to their rescue.[12]

Ten years past, the Yanktonai Dakota and Sitting Bull's Hunkpapa Lakota would have struck terror in all who passed by Dogden Butte. Sitting Bull was a frequent hunter in this area. The Sioux made peace with the Métis in the mid-1860s. It is likely Gardipee encountered him and hunted the buffalo with his people within the Mouse River loop in the 1870s.[13]

The U.S. military pacified the Dakota and Lakota peoples in 1877, but in the past, they had been the enemies of all. Dogden Butte was the frontier between the Assiniboine to the north and west, the Yanktonai Dakota to the south, the Mandan/Hidatsa to the south and west and the Plains Ojibwa and Plains Cree to the northeast. The Hunkpapa Lakota lived south and west of the Missouri. In the old days, travel to the Mandan trading villages from the north and east involved passing by Dogden, a perfect location for an ambush. For centuries, this was a place of violence and death between the warring tribes of the northern Great Plains.

In the 1700s and early 1800s, French Canadian Nor'Westers like Gardipee's father, Louis, and uncle Francis[14] came to Red River / Pembina River country seeking furs. Marriage brought them into a relationship with the Ojibwa and the Cree. The offspring of the French Nor'Westers became the Métis Nation. The Métis, Ojibwa, Cree and Assiniboine formed an alliance called the Nehiyaw Pwat, also known as the Iron Alliance. They wanted to ensure that they alone would be the go-between with the English Hudson Bay Company in the trade of iron objects like guns, hatchets, kettles and arrowheads. They controlled the fur trade in the Northwest for one hundred years up into the 1860s and were constantly at war with the Sioux.

Dogden was a prominent landmark used by travelers in ancient Dakota history. It rises two hundred feet from the edge of the drift prairie. Anyone approaching from the north and east can see it for miles. It is also a historical reference point mentioned and visited by a lengthy line of well-known, lesser-known and unknown characters of the Old West. Verendrye,

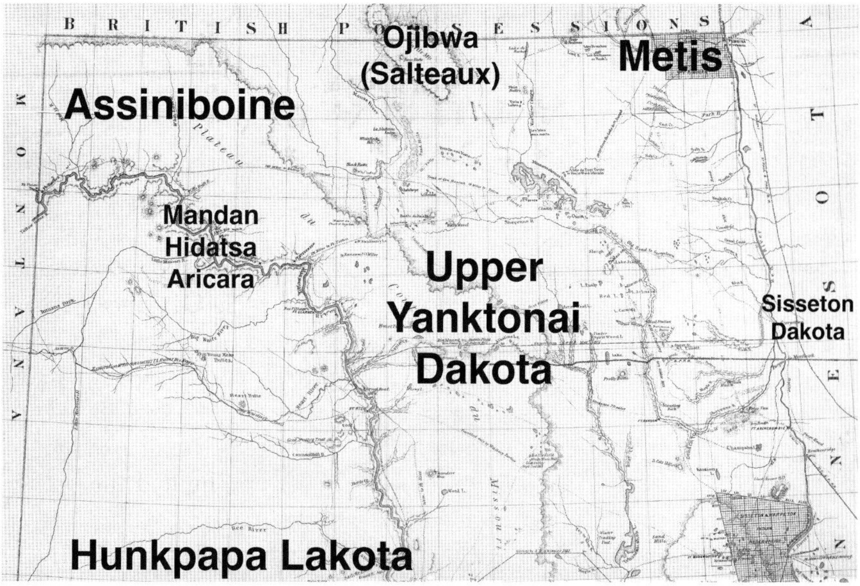

Territory of Native American tribes about 1870 on Rice's Sectional Map of 1876. *Library of Congress.*

David Thompson, Charbonneau and other voyagers and traders from the Hudson Bay Company and the Nor'Westers passed this way. Sitting Bull, Inkpaduta, Medicine Bear, De Trobriand, George Custer, Kootenai Brown, Vic Smith, Yellowstone Kelly and nameless trappers, wolfers, buffalo hunters, Montana gold miners, wagon trains, cowboys, cattle drives, horse thieves, vigilantes, lawmen and Pony Express riders worked, passed through, visited or died here.

Grieving Change

As dangerous as those times were, Gardipee longingly dreamed of them. It was an era of abundant plenty. What glory and wealth the Métis people enjoyed. In contrast, a painful sadness had settled on the Native peoples of the Great Plains. Change came to the heart and home of the Métis with soul-ripping rapidity. From the late 1860s through the 1870s up to 1882, the only people living along the Mouse River were the few small settlements of Métis and their Plains Ojibwa cousins. The principal part of the Red River Bison herd disappeared in mystery and shocking suddenness in the winter of 1867.[15]

Through the 1870s, the Métis still hunted the dwindling remnant of the Red River herd in the Mouse River loop.[16] Only a smattering of buffalo was left by 1880. In all the years of Gardipee's youth, these prairies produced an abundance. Thousands of lakes and wetlands dot the landscape, creating the nesting grounds of the North American waterfowl population.[17] Ducks, geese, swans, sandhill cranes and plovers provided a ready source of food at any point all spring, summer and fall. The crackling call of red-winged blackbirds, the melodious song of the meadowlark, the cooing of mourning dove, the quack of a Suzy mallard and the braying and honking of geese fill the empty prairie with sound.

A carpet of mixed-grass prairie blanketed these hills. In a transition zone between the tallgrass prairies of the Red River Valley and the shortgrass prairies in the more arid regions to the west, this plant community is a mixture of each. Big bluestem, switchgrass and Indian grass dominated the tallgrass prairie. It stood as tall as a man in many places. In Dogden country, you would find the tall grasses around the sloughs, but across the hills, there was a carpet about a foot high of needle grass, side oats gramma, wheatgrass, needle and thread grass and the purple-red clumps of little bluestem. Many wildflowers, legumes and weeds were mixed in with the grass. The tops of the hills had shorter grasses like blue gamma and buffalo grass.

It was nutritious and hardy, the perfect pasture for the millions of bison, pronghorn antelope and Manitoba elk that grazed on it. Their hides and meat had been the source of the Métis people's significant wealth. Beginning in the 1880s, this pasture became filled with cows and horses.

THAT DAMN WIND

Trees were so rare that where they occurred, the Métis referred to them as an island—a small island of safety and protection from the rolling sea of wind-swept grassland. The weather is brutal. It gets so cold that the cats sleep on top of dogs. Winters begin early and remain long.[18] Temperatures at -35 to -40 degrees happen most winters. Exposed skin freezes in minutes in this kind of weather. People caught out walking in the open without proper clothing in a Dakota blizzard will die. Summers can be hot and dry or cold and wet. Periodic drought plagues the area. Violent lightning and thunderstorms, hailstorms and tornadoes are annual occurrences. The river valleys are also subject to periodic flooding.

But the most prominent feature of these prairies was and still is the wind. That damn wind![19] It never stops. A wintry day becomes bitter cold and deadly because of wind chills, which have reached the extreme of -83 degrees. Only the calm day is worth a mention.

In 1882, that damn icy wind blew a new and forever change into the homes of the Métis on the Mouse River.

HACKETT

In the fall of 1881, Edmund Hackett was exploring possible railway routes through the Mouse River country. He was also searching for that perfect town site. He stumbled upon Gardipee's log hamlet on the Mouse River. On property next to Francis and Caroline Gardipee's place, he founded Souris City (nicknamed Hackett Falls). Upriver a few miles, Hackett wrote the name "Villard" on a stake and drove it into the ground. Another frontier village was born.

During the winter/spring of 1882, Hackett returned with an entire expedition of Americans and Norwegians into the Mouse River valley. Many of these people remained as settlers, camping and claiming land up and downriver near Gardipee's home.[20] They immediately began building houses and stores. Hackett staked out three claims: a homestead, a tree-claim and a preemption claim. The preemption claim included the land on which Gardipee had squatted years ago.[21] Conflict was brewing; a showdown with Hackett was inevitable. Gardipee had good reason not to trust him. It was soon obvious that Hackett thought himself superior to Gardipee and his Métis family and friends.

The Wendigo is a legendary creature prominent in the folklore of the Cree (the people of Gardipee's mother). They believed that if a human being tasted human flesh, that person would slowly turn into a Wendigo monster with an insatiable appetite for more flesh. The greed consumed them until they no longer resembled humans at all. Gardipee may have wondered about Hackett and what kind of monster he would become, with such a voracious hunger for power and fortune.

THE FIRST CATTLE DRIVE

One year after the establishment of Villard, in August 1883, the Pendroy clan arrived at the Mouse River valley with three hundred head of shorthorn cows, whiteface Hereford bulls and some mixed breed cattle. They had been in the cattle business near Marion County, Iowa. This family had raised Herefords for generations. Open grazing land in Iowa was falling to the plow, so this extended family headed out in May 1883. It was Yankee Robinson, a plainsman and Hudson Bay Company trapper who had lived and worked the Mouse River valley since the early 1860s, who invited the Pendroy clan to Mouse River country. The Pendroys met him in Bismarck on an exploratory trip in 1882, looking for the best place to bring their cattle.[22]

For seventy-five days, they trailed their herd north from Iowa along the Missouri River. Theirs were the first cattle driven into the Mouse River valley and the first Herefords east of the Missouri. The Pendroys launched what would be twenty years of open-range cattle ranching that dominated Mouse River / Dogden Butte country as it did the prairies throughout the Old West. That summer, on the heels of the Pendroy clan, came more settlers with more horses and cattle.[23]

Mouse River Cattle Drive, 1883 (Thursby herd). *Collection:10147 Folder: 0007.000 Item: 0008 SHSND.*

Temptation

As Gardipee and his dogs flew along the snow-encrusted hills toward Washburn, it is likely he was wrestling with his conscience. Raised in the Catholic faith, he had been catechized by Jesuits in Sunday school classes conducted under the Red River carts on the open prairies during summer buffalo hunts. He believed in "Thou Shall Not Steal" and lived under this law written on his heart. But in the summer of 1883, a close friend, Bruneau (Burno),[24] and acquaintances, Aleck Brown, Caribo Fountaine and Pierre Hannery, had been talking about taking advantage of the resources of cattle and horses newly brought into their home territory. They were likely recruited by Dutch Charley and probably sending the stock through his camp by Turtle Mountain. Some had already started this enterprise in the fall of 1883, with substantial success. It was easy to do and, given their difficult circumstances, easy for the Métis to justify.

The Red River buffalo hunt ended in the 1870s. The last of the massive Montana buffalo herd disappeared in 1882. Other big game—deer, elk and antelope—were getting harder to find as well. Unfamiliar people were taking over the land claimed by the Métis Nation. Land hard-won in battle from the Sioux, held by the Iron Alliance, was occupied and exploited.

These uninvited rich newcomers could spare a few head of stock; many Métis families were perishing. In some places, the Indigenous Plains people were dying of starvation because of the recent loss of the buffalo with nothing to replace it. Perhaps these new settlers owed some of these cattle and horses to the Métis.[25] They should give something for this land.

Bruneau and Brown were not persons of exemplary character.[26] But it would be hard to ignore Gardipee's friends' request for help. It would be easy to steal horses from these recent arrivals. The new settlers were ignorant of the lay of the land and all the back trails and hidden coulees where stock could be secreted away. All they needed to do was to get the stolen animals across the Medicine Line—that magical, invisible space beyond which American soldiers and authorities would not pursue an Indian. They would need help to hold the stock out in the sand hills near Gardipee's home or in the deep draws of Dogden Butte. Once the thieves collected a sizable herd, they could run it up into Canada to sell.

GARDIPEE'S CHANGE OF HEART

In August 1884, Gardipee was caught driving stolen horses headed to the border. Why? What changed him from an honest man making a place for himself with the people of Villard into one of the horse thieves? He brought the mail by horseback in the fall until the snows got too deep, then by dogsled over the prairies from Washburn. Late that fall, Gardipee placed stakes every three hundred yards in stretches where he might lose the trail.[27]

His service as a mail carrier that winter of 1884 almost cost him his life. This had been a particularly severe winter. It happened on February 11; the temperature that day was at -28 degrees. As Gardipee set out in the morning on the return trip from Washburn to Pendroy and Villard, the snow

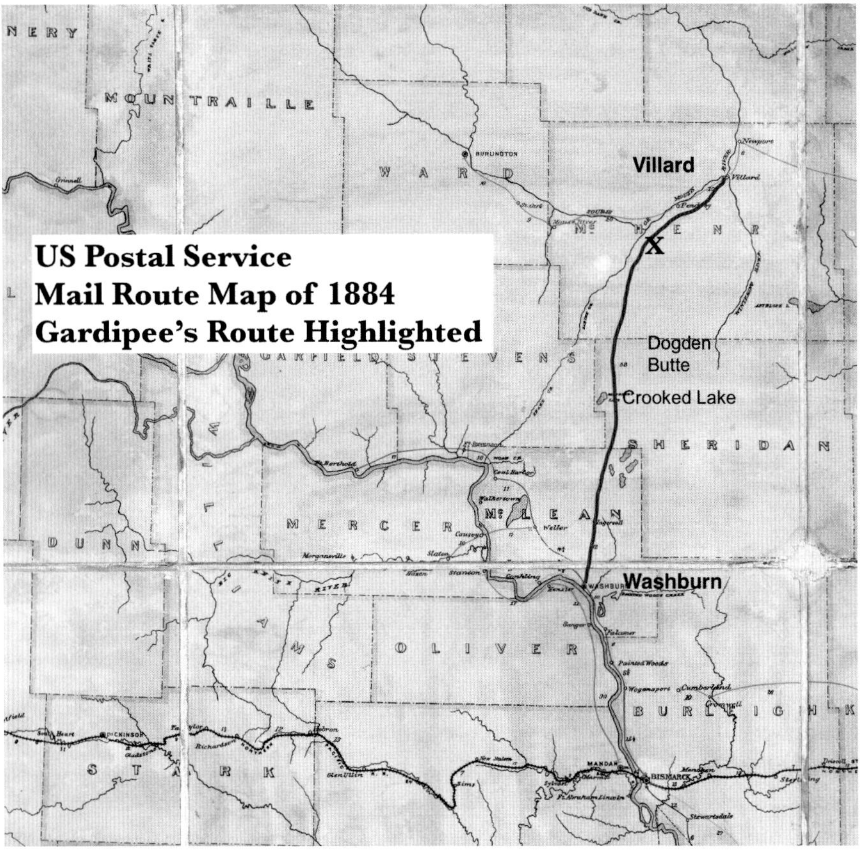

Gardipee's 1884 mail route. The X marks location of night in snowbank (approximate). *David Rumsey Map Collection, David Rumsey Map Center, Stanford Libraries.*

fell. The wind kicked up from the northwest until everything—the sky and the ground—turned to white. Gardipee pressed on, trusting his dogs to find the way, watching for the stakes that marked the trail. Over the hours, as he pressed forward, the reflected light off the snow burned the corneas of his eyes. The damage became so severe that he was soon nearly blind.[28] He was in danger of drifting off the trail and becoming hopelessly lost in the night. The storm was getting stronger. It forced him to make camp. Camp consisted of a cave dug out of a snowbank and curling up in his wool blanket with no fire.

In the morning, frozen and hungry, he scratched out of the snow only to discover his dogs had abandoned him. Almost completely without sight, he was forced to leave the sled and mail and stumble afoot the remaining six miles to Pendroy.[29] Recovering from snow blindness laid Gardipee up for weeks. While he was convalescing, his job as a mail carrier was given to someone else. Could this unfortunate turn of luck explain how this heretofore honest man joined in with the horse thieves the following summer?

REFLECTION

Gardipee must have seen the morning sunrise over Maison Du Chien countless times. He might have recalled the stories of the Mandan People about this place. They, like Gardipee, were spiritual people. They were aware of the spiritual forces at work over these prairies, buttes and lakes. Shadow rulers that humanity must respect, the watchers of the millennia over the earth, are in the land and even in the wind.

In the atheistic worldview that dominates our media and academia in America today, there is only this material world, only one tier. The Enlightenment Christian worldview recognized two tiers. They believed in the tier of heaven where God dwells and the tier of this physical world where humans dwell. But in the Christianity of the Bible and the experience of the animistic peoples of the world, there is a third tier. It is what some call the missing middle.[30] This is the realm between heaven and earth, a dimension where spiritual beings interact with the human world. It is a shadow of the physical earth. The Bible calls it the heavenlies.[31] To believers of many stripes around the world, a multitude of spirits, both good and evil, inhabit this middle realm. The Native American peoples saw their universe in this way, as would Gardipee.

Dogden Butte today. *Photo by Eric Berget Carpe Season Photography.*

The Mandan Indian people gave Dogden Butte (Mashugadish) its name. To the Mandan, Dog's Den is a place of great spiritual importance. Their religious myths capture the spiritual tenor of this place and reflect their experience of a spirit influence on the physical land.

The Mandan mythical story of Dogden Mountain is this: "A woman mated with a dog and produced boy dogs. They were separated from their mother by a windy storm. The youngest boy dog led their mother to their den on this butte and this has been called Dogs Den ever since."

The Mandan myths include a Christ figure named Lone Man, a great flood, a great canoe and other archetypes that transcend all human cultures. Heroes and tricksters inhabit the myths of most of humanity. The battle between good and evil, the source of that evil, the meaning of good and why it is so elusive to humans were questions for the Mandan people on this land, the European immigrants who came to live here over the last 150 years and the new peoples who will follow in the centuries to come. People come and go, but our questions remain throughout the generations.

Gardipee may also have struggled with that question. Why had God, who so abundantly blessed and protected the Métis for one hundred years, abandoned them and turned this land over to an unfamiliar people? What had the Métis done to offend him? This land, indwelt by spiritual forces and swept by that damned chilling wind, is a backdrop for human drama that time plays out repeatedly. These Old West stories are timeless tales of human suffering and failure, of descent from order to chaos and back, only to repeat the cycle. Humanity is lost and in need of redemption. Humanity needs a Lone Man.

Nothing changed on this landscape for millennia. The same people lived here for hundreds of years. But in 1492, a new era of global exploration began. The European world and this American world collided. The change came, slowly at first and then faster and faster. In the late eighteenth century, a new people group emerged from this land. The Métis are a product of the mixture of these two worlds. From this new mixed ethnicity came a new family—the Gariepys (Gardipees). These people lived for eighty years amid plenty. They sang, they danced, they hunted and they prayed. And God blessed them, and they multiplied, but now it seemed their time was coming to a bitter end.

2

EDMUND HACKETT

The Crony Capitalist

If talent, good looks, athletic ability and connections make a man successful and rich, then Edmund Hackett should have died wealthy, powerful and loved by all. He had these qualities in abundance. They were not enough. A sadder tale of reversal of fortune would be hard to find. His life demonstrates gifts are no substitute for character.

Early Years

Hackett was born in 1833 in Bombay, New York, twelve miles from the Canadian border.[32] It was a town of 1,700 people. His parents were Irish immigrants. He was the oldest of four children. William Wheeler, a close

Edmund Hackett. The only photo of Hackett is of poor quality from the *Bismarck Tribune*, April 7, 1934. This artist's depiction is based on that photo. *Sketch by Sarah Johannsen.*

The Battle of Secessionville. *Courtesy of the South Caroliniana Library, University of South Carolina, Columbia, SC.*

childhood friend and neighbor, became vice president of the United States. (Hackett stayed in touch with this friend to some political advantage.)[33] When only a teen, Edmund was required to step up to become the man of his home when his father died.[34] At age twenty-two, he married Bridget Ward, an Irish Catholic girl. Hackett spent his twenties in Manchester, New Hampshire, laboring as a blacksmith in the rapidly growing industrial city. There he and Bridget had their first children, Edmund Jr. and John. A daughter, Mary, would come a few years later.

The Civil War began on April 12, 1861, when Jeff Davis ordered his generals to attack Fort Sumter. That summer, the Third New Hampshire Regiment was formed, and Hackett enlisted, at age twenty-eight, on July 10 in the first muster. They assigned him to serve in Company C under Captain Donohoe as a wagoner. Company C was almost entirely native-born Irish. The Third New Hampshire and Company C saw some real action one year later: June 1862, at the Battle of Secessionville, laying siege to Charleston, South Carolina. Many in the Third New Hampshire became sick that year, and this may be the reason the army discharged Edmond Hackett in September 1862 after only one year of a three-year enlistment.[35]

A New Trade and New Opportunities

After the Civil War, Edmund Hackett moved his family to Missouri, and there he became a carpenter. He learned balloon framing, which was replacing the post and beam method. Balloon framing was faster, simpler and could be done with unskilled labor. Contractors could put up wooden structures quickly by whatever labor was at hand. This was what was needed to throw up the boomtowns in the Old West.

In 1870, Walter Burleigh invited Hackett, age thirty-seven, to apply his craft at Burleigh Crossing on the Missouri. Hackett constructed the first permanent wood-frame building in what would soon be Bismarck, Dakota Territory.[36] He also helped with the construction of Fort Rice and Fort Abraham Lincoln—the home of George Custer.[37]

Hackett stayed here with his family, and his dreams and aspirations grew with the country. There were great fortunes to be made from the expansion into the West. Bismarck was for Hackett, as with so many others, that next great opportunity. Edmund Hackett was almost successful many times over. In fact, had he stuck with working as a building contractor, his story would likely have ended better. But unfortunately, he, like the state he helped to create, would try to do too much.[38]

A tall and handsome man, Hackett had an outgoing personality, his black hair at times grown long in the plainsman style, reaching to his shoulders.[39] He developed ambitions toward political influence and power, and he possessed the right set of gifts to achieve this.

POLITICAL ASPIRATION

In 1873, Bismarck elected Hackett constable of a lawless western town very much in need of cleaning up. Colonel Lounsbury, the editor of Bismarck's first newspaper, shares his remembrance of what this Old West railroad town was like in 1872 and 1873. The description moves down the street in the photograph on the next page. The account reads like an Old West movie script.[40]

> *The White building afterwards became the Sam Whitney opera house, and standing in its door Jack Richards killed Frank Cole with as much coolness as a Fargo sportsman would wing a chicken. Beside this building Paddy Hall stood when he shot Jack O'Neil, who was gunning for him.*
>
> *Next was the "Hole in the Wall" kept by George Bridges, and along there somewhere was Chris Hehli's barber shop. E.A. Williams had an office in the Ed. Hackett building. Near that was another saloon building and then where McLean & MacNider afterwards built was a huge tent for gambling purposes, and on the corner the old Merchants Hotel, before Griffin took it, used as a gambling hall, and by its side the Minnehaha saloon.*

Bismarck, Dakota Territory, 1873. A rough-and-tumble Old West railroad town. *Collection: C Folder: 0000.000 Item: 0529 00004 SHSND.*

The first church organized in North Dakota was in this tent. W.H. White of Fargo, Colonel Lounsberry of The Record, John W. Fisher and H.F. Douglas took part in the meeting. The gambling halls and saloons all closed their places during service, and the town was as quiet as a camp meeting.

Around the corner, back of the old Merchants, "Yellow Hammer," a Mexican greaser, had a shack, W.H. Comer, born of slave parents, who descended from a family of slaves, owned by George Washington, had a shop. Scott & Millett had a livery stable and there were other small shacks now almost forgotten.

On the corner where the Merchants Bank stood, the 25-foot lot selling in 1882 for $8,000, was Mullen & O'Neill's dance hall. There was wine, women, cards, anything that corrupt men or bad women would be apt to seek, was on tap, so to speak. Spotty Whalen, associated with the place, killed a soldier at the "Point" in the fall of 1873, and the soldiers raided the town and killed Mullen and shot Monahan, his bartender, Mullen killing one or two of the soldiers while they were firing a whole volley at him.

Later Sally O'Neill died a violent death, her "man" being Mullen's partner, and their bookkeeper was killed by John Richards, and O'Neill by Paddy Hall, as mentioned above. In all there were seven murders connected with this establishment, and when Judge Barnes was called upon to hold court in a building on this street, he refused because of its terrible record of blood.

Next to Mullen & O'Neill's was the Seventh Cavalry saloon, as tough as tough could be, kept by Chris Gilson, an old frontiersman, who had followed the Seventh Cavalry for many years and was last heard from playing the role of a "refugee" who escaped from the Custer massacre, though not in it.

Jack Champlin's bawdy house was next on the list and then Pat Gallagher's and various other saloons and gambling houses in one of which Brooks was killed. Brooks was with one of the expeditions out west and leaving the camp one morning about sixty-five miles out, he announced his intention to take supper in Bismarck or hell that night. He got to Bismarck and was soon afterwards killed in a building owned by Dennis Hannafin. Dennis knew the murder would hoo doo the building and cut short his bar receipts for some days to come. He spared no expense, however, to entertain the corpse and gave it the grandest wake that any jolly frontiersman ever had and rendered the bill to the estate and it was paid. Twenty-five years is a long time to remember incidents and buildings in detail, but it was also on this block where Pete Brannigan killed his man, where "Short and Dirty," "Be Jesus Lize," "Big Maria," "Thumbs Up" and other notorious characters, not to speak of "Big Mary," then known as Mary Gilson, plied their vocation.

Constable Hackett, along with the others in the local police force, did clean up the town. In the fall of 1873, Hackett accompanied Spotty Whalen east for trial in protective custody, so Whalen wouldn't be murdered by the Seventh Cavalry. Libby Custer arrived from St. Paul with her husband to move into the newly constructed Fort Abraham Lincoln. Libby said the local constables met her and George at the train station with all the outlaws of Bismarck, rounded up to be sent east on the last train out of town before the winter of 1873–74.[41]

Constable was the first step in a rapidly rising political career in the new territory. Hackett was climbing a ladder to power and influence and the privilege he hoped it would bring. Next step was to serve as a clerk on Bismarck's first school board and then on to bigger things. In 1874, Hackett ran for a spot as a Democrat in the Territorial Legislature. This election was a breeze, as his opponent was in jail for murder. However, at the legislative session in Yankton, the clerk read the wrong name and installed the accused murderer William T. McKay in this seat by accident. They released McKay from jail when he needed to vote as instructed.[42]

To placate Hackett's disappointment, his political friends appointed him the first mayor of Bismarck, Dakota Territory. But alas, he lost that job to

John McLean in the May 1875 election. In 1876, there was finally some success. He ran for the House in the Dakota Territorial Legislature and won; he served two terms.

Hackett seemed always to be angling to make a buck. The *Bismarck Tribune* is replete with stories of Hackett in the courts over land disputes. He also played a key role in the city of Mandan's establishment.[43]

Railroad Speculation

In 1874, Colonel George Armstrong Custer, departing from Fort Abraham Lincoln, led an expedition of one thousand men into the Black Hills of Dakota Territory. Its purpose was to determine if the rumors were true about gold there. The Laramie Treaty of 1868 established that this land belonged to the Lakota people. Custer's expedition violated that treaty. They found gold, and nothing could stop the onslaught of miners with gold fever. This resulted in the Great Sioux War and Custer's famous Last Stand. The war was brief, the Lakota defeated, and the miners poured into the Black Hills.

Hackett and his Yankee capitalist cronies looked for a way to exploit this latest gold rush. He and other speculators chartered the Bismarck, Fort Lincoln and Black Hills Railroad in 1877. With the nation still in recession, they could not find the needed investors. They then sought to establish the Bismarck to Lake Kampeska (northeast South Dakota) Railroad in 1878, but again, the project failed.

Hackett tried a third time in 1881 to organize the Bismarck, Mouse River, Turtle Mountain and Manitoba Railroad Company. Board members included Erastus Williams, Alexander McKenzie, John P. Dunn and James A. Emmons. North Dakotans will recognize those as the names of four western North Dakota counties. Williams was president and McKenzie general manager. They raised $2 million in capital. The proposed route ran 180 miles north from Bismarck past Dogden Butte, along the Mouse River and on the west side of Turtle Mountain and connecting with communities growing on the Canadian side of the international border. The proposed track followed that ancient trail—the Road to the Mandan—and promised to give it a new life.

They wasted no time moving ahead with the project. In the fall of 1881, Hackett picked out two town sites on the Mouse River that would be likely spots the Northern Pacific would connect with their railroad and cross the river. Here he staked his claim and future hopes of fortune.[44]

Founding Villard

That winter of 1882, Hackett organized an exploratory expedition[45] that his friends publicized in the *Bismarck Tribune*, sending back what could only be described as propaganda to promote the country they hoped to exploit. The entire endeavor beautifully captured the feelings and excitement of the times: new lands, new opportunities, being on the ground floor of a "can't miss" venture. It was manifest destiny at its best and, as we shall see, its worst.

Hackett's vision was spot-on correct. He knew someone was going to land on just the right place and a major city would grow. It all depended on the flow of commerce, the junction of the roads, the railroads and the river. Minot, today a city of forty thousand people, was in the right spot. Hackett was betting he found that sweet spot.

> *Six of the exploring party return, report that country a daisy. Six of the Mouse river explorers…returned Tuesday afternoon. From Mr. Campbell the TRIBUNE gained many facts of interest regarding that country. The town site of Villard has been laid out on ex-Mayor Hackett's claim, embracing 320 acres.*

Campbell also laid out on the table at the *Tribune* a twenty-pound northern pike that he had taken from the Mouse River. In that first year, they shipped five thousand fish to market in Bismarck from the Mouse River. The Métis who also lived along the Mouse River caught thousands more to feed the Ojibwa at Turtle Mountain.

In February, Hackett sent back his first report via Jewell, the vice president of the railroad, who published it in the *Tribune*:

> *Sir: I have the honor of submitting to you the following report: I sent you a brief dispatch from Dog Den mountain, and as stated in that I found an easy pass through those ranges of hills. I reached Villard on the 24th inst. The country from the Dog Den to Villard is somewhat rolling, and beautifully watered with lakes and streams. Their banks are well timbered with ash and white birch. Wintering river runs through this valley, and heads to the southeast in the Coteaus, running northwest and emptying into the Mouse river at the big bend. This valley is large…from 30 to 40 miles wide, with a fertile soil of black loam with clay subsoil. Thousands of homesteads can be located here. By Ed Hackett.*

Hackett's exploration continued up the Mouse River valley. His report drips with optimism and excitement:

> *I find it to be the most beautiful country the sun ever shone on. A level prairie, stretching away as far as the eye can reach, with the exception of Turtle Mountain here in front of me on the east, the country, rolling to the Mousey is dotted with lakes and small groves of timber, and tall grasses of every variety. The varieties of timber growing on Turtle mountain are of a valuable kind.... The trees grow tall and thrifty, and from two to three feet in thickness. This timber is very much needed in the growing northwest and it is a prize worth contending for. Turtle mountain seems to be very extensive, and looks to an observer somewhat like the Black Hills, and no doubt contains minerals.*[46]
>
> *The Mouse river valley is larger than the Red river valley of the north, is better watered and timbered, and better adapted to stock raising. A railroad from Bismarck can be built on the proposed route at a comparatively trifling cost. No heavy grade to overcome, nothing but the level and fertile prairie to run over. Ties can be procured in quantities sufficient along its line to tie the road bed.*
>
> *A word to the merchants and capitalists of Bismarck, and that is, invest your surplus cash in this road. It will pay 99 cents on the dollar. Open this great gateway of commerce to your doors. Think of your geographical location. Situated on the greatest navigable stream on this continent, crossed at your city—by the great transcontinental railway, the North Pacific. The construction of the Bismarck, Mouse River, Turtle Mountain and Manitoba road will be a competing line with the whole western system of transportation. Grain can be shipped over that line from Winnipeg to Bismarck thence loaded on steamboats and run to the gulf by river, and from there to all parts of Europe. Is this not more practicable than the Hudson Bay route? The Mouse River is settled up to the line on the Manitoba side, and I am informed that some families have come on this side of the line and have made permanent settlements. They are now as near Bismarck as they are to their own capitol.*[47]

These are the words of a big-picture visionary. Details be damned, we can do this. All we need is your money. Bismarck lost contact with Hackett's party that spring, and concerned friends almost sent for the troops from Fort Stevenson to search for them when they drifted back into town in April. Deep snow and that cursed wind trapped them for a time. But the long winter did not chill their spirits as they made the most of their extended stay.

The anxiety regarding the fate of ex-Mayor Hackett's party of Mouse river explorers is happily over. Mr. Hackett and several members of his party returned Tuesday. Mr. Hackett, who will remain at Bismarck in order to lead an expedition from here to Mouse river on May 1st, is more than ever infatuated with that rich agricultural valley. The party during their snow blockade was not at all idle, but were busy in making improvements. Several new houses were built in Villard and on adjacent claims.[48]

Leah Hortense Youngs

Bridget Hackett died in April 1883 at age forty-nine. Hundreds attended her funeral, evidence of the prominent place the Hacketts had in the Bismarck community.[49]

Shortly after Bridget's death, Edmund Hackett noticed an attractive stage actress from New York City performing at the Bismarck Opera House. Her stage name was Frankie Sydney, and Hackett managed an introduction. Her given name was Leah Hortense Youngs. With Hackett fifty years old in 1883 and Leah just twenty, she was about the same age as his daughter, Mary.

These must have felt like the best of times for Hackett. He was garnering recognition and becoming an influential person—1883 was a fantastic year. He planted two towns, established the new McHenry County and would soon appoint himself its first county commissioner—not to mention being part of an exciting new railroad startup company. Maybe it was not so surprising that a young woman might view this wealthy man to be as fair a catch as she might find. And for a man in mid-life, what better way to be impressed with yourself than the interest of a woman thirty years younger that every other man would wish to have? A trophy wife, I believe we call them today. Yes, Edmund Hackett had every reason to feel very proud.

The towns of Villard and Hackett Falls (also known as Souris City) were pregnant with possibilities in 1883. But embarrassingly, so was Leah. This was the Victorian era. Leah's pregnancy came about three months after Bridget's death, and they quickly planned a wedding. Hackett made a brief announcement after the fact in the *Bismarck Tribune* on December 13, 1883:

Hackett—Youngs—at the Custer House.
Monday. December 10 at the Custer House. Rev. J.G. Miller. Edmund Hackett and Leah Hortense Youngs, both of Bismarck.

The Sam Whitney Opera House Bismarck, DT. Note young actress on stage. Woodcut from *Harper's Weekly*. *Collection: E Folder: 0000.000 Item: 0430 00001 SHSND.*

Edmund purchased land at Minnewaukan on the west shoreline of Devils Lake. It was a beautiful spot, remote, where Leah could go to have her baby out of the sight of all the folks in Bismarck and Villard. The baby boy was born in April. Edmund split his time between Bismarck, Souris City and the sixty-mile trip to their Minnewaukan getaway.

HACKETT'S PREJUDICE

Edmund Hackett's last report from Turtle Mountain reveals the evil side to manifest destiny and relates directly to Gardipee and his family. It reveals the racism and ill feelings toward those who had been here for a century before. I will let Ed Hackett show you himself:

> *Mr. Jewell As I stated to you in the above report that I would start next day for Turtle mountain, I wish to inform you that I have accomplished the journey after four days of hard traveling…Some sixty miles to the half-breed settlement on the east side of the mountain.*
>
> *When first we struck the settlement or village, we were saluted with the howling of about fifty half-starved dogs. The village is scattered over some three or four hundred acres, the building, or dwellings consist of small log huts, and the balance are of the tepee style, made of skins and on the whole has a dilapidated appearance. Each family has a patch of about an acre under cultivation which comprises their farms.*[50]

Hackett met the leader, Black Bear, who invited him into his tepee and fed him.

> *He is not a full-blooded Indian. After the pipe was handed round, supper was ordered and was gotten up on short notice, consisting of Mouse river fish, hard bread and coffee. I asked him if he was the head chief of the Turtle mountain band of Chippewas. He answered no, the head chief he said lived at Woody Mountain, on the other side of the line. I asked why he did not live there with his tribe. He said the chief became disgusted here with his people and would not live with them. He also stated that the chief at Woody Mountain held the papers from the president for these lands. I asked him how they proposed to dispose of these lands, and learned that the half-breeds wanted a reservation sixty miles long and fifty miles wide, and*

The Totten Trail by Henry Farny. This is like the Ojibway village described by Hackett. *Public domain.*

> *a certain sum of money to the chiefs. I told him that I did not believe the government would give a reservation to half-breeds, but that they could take a hundred and sixty acres, the same as a white man, under the homestead and pre-emption law, he answered and said that the half breeds should have a reservation as the white men had all the money. I asked him what he thought about going to the White Earth reservation, and he said they would not go anywhere until they got pay for their lands, and then they could go where they pleased. This ended the conversation for the evening, and he kindly procured us a lodge for the night.*

There is more to this than we have space to develop in this book. It is part of a much larger story of the Plains Ojibwa, the Métis and their fight for a place. The Gardipee family were members of the Turtle Mountain Band of the Chippewa. Some mixed-race people identified more as Native Americans and took Native American names. Some, like Gardipee, identified more as Europeans.[51] Now you see them through the eyes of Edmund Hackett. He continues his report:

> *During my stay I had looked the matter over carefully, and I find not a full-blooded Chippewa in this tribe, called the Turtle Mountain band of Chippewas. They are nothing but a renegade set of half-breeds from the various tribes of northern and Canadian Indians. There is not over two hundred and fifty souls all in this so-called band of Turtle Mountain Indians. They are settled here in this remote part of our territory on the boundary line. They are the outfit that have been furnishing Sitting Bull and his band of cutthroats and murderers with ammunition and guns, during all our frontier troubles, and now they are perched on this mountain, on the boundary line, ready to jump from one side or the other as the case may be and after all this they have the cheek to ask the government for a*

reservation sixty miles wide and fifty long, the best lands of Dakota. People do not know the wealth that is to be found here. Very little of it is known to the outside world. Eighteen months ago it would not have been safe for a white man to put his foot on this soil, but since the surrender of Sitting Bull the white man can travel with perfect safety. I will start for Villard in a day or two, as soon as our stock has recuperated a little. Ed Hackett.[52]

CHRISTMAS CHEER 1883

Christmas 1883 was a carefree time for the Hackett couple on their honeymoon at the lake house on Devils Lake and with a baby on the way. However, Hackett's luck would not hold. Within one year, everything would change. That damned wind would blow a chill over everyone in 1884. We must wait to see the hardest luck of all that comes in the Christmas of 1884. You already know it will be a bad Christmas for the Gardipee family. A frozen prairie lake near Dogden Butte locked Francis's cold, lifeless body in

A ranch on the Mouse River in the 1880s. Hackett's place may have looked like this. *Collection: 10147 Folder: 0007.000 Item: 00003 SHSND.*

its grip. But Edmund Hackett faced the darkest Christmas of his life too. We will finish those stories in chapter 9.

There is one more character we must get to know. He spent Christmas 1883 spying on the horse thief camps along the Missouri in Montana. Circumstances would bring these three together for the deadly events of November 1884.

3

FLOPPING BILL CANTRELL

Plainsman / Thief Killer

The Plainsmen of Dogden Butte

The plainsmen were those first American adventurers who made the western prairies home and became the vanguard of all the others who would eventually fill in the wilderness west of the Mississippi. They arrived during the fur trade era, before 1870. They are true icons of western history and lore.

The most famous plainsmen are Buffalo Bill Cody and Wild Bill Hickok. But they did not live in Dogden Butte country. Here in central North Dakota, we had the likes of Yellowstone Kelly, Kootenai Brown, Joseph Taylor and Vic Smith. We know a little something about these men because of the books they wrote. Some, like Yellowstone Kelly and

Flopping Bill, stock detective. Sketch based on a photo in *Kaleidoscope Lives* by Joseph Taylor. *Sketch by Sarah Johannsen.*

Kootenai Brown, have had their stories retold in movies.[53] There couldn't have been more than a few hundred others in the upper Missouri region, and most left little mark on history.

BIG BILL CANTRELL

In the late 1860s, Kootenai Brown and a Métis man named Gardipee were running Pony Express mail routes out of Fort Stevenson. At this same time, another youthful man found his way north into the Upper Missouri country and into the life of a plainsman. A mere twenty years old when he arrived, William Cantrell came seeking fortune, the romance of the wilderness and the challenge of an unknown land. Bill was a southerner, born in 1848 in Tennessee, and raised in Arkansas.[54] He was from a family of teens and young adults orphaned by the war who split up in 1866.[55] Bill headed north and west to become a true plainsman, and an infamous legend at that. He, like so many others, got his introduction to the plainsman lifestyle in north-central Dakota Territory.

John R. Barrows described Flopping Bill as "over six feet, bony, muscular, slow moving, with a bearing of combined reticence and dignity." Barrows called him "an Ironside," but, he said, "I did not detect the Bible."[56] Likely Bill was, like most plainsmen and cowboys, an atheist or at least not a practitioner of religion. Many who chose this lifestyle did so to get away from organized religion. Teddy Blue, Granville Stuart, Kootenai Brown, Vic Smith and Joseph Taylor all make this clear in their writings. They all shared a real disdain for churches and religious leaders.

QUANTRILL'S RAIDERS

Bill Cantrell often said that his father was a relative of William Quantrill of Quantrill's Raiders.[57] He also said his father fought with Quantrill in the Civil War. Quantrill's Raiders were a Confederate guerrilla army famed for their many atrocities committed during the war. Bill Cantrell claimed he was present when one of the worst of these occurred in Lawrence, Kansas. They murdered 150 men and boys. The Raiders executed them unarmed.[58] This story, that Bill fought with Quantrill, came from Bill himself, according to Joseph Taylor.

The steamer *Josephine* (1873–1907), a Missouri riverboat. *Collection: 20406 Folder: 0000.000 Item: 00003 SHSND.*

> *He exploited the deeds of his sire as one of Quantrill's men and intimated that notwithstanding his own youthful appearance he too had followed that bold guerilla chief on his Kansas raid that ended in the sacking of Lawrence.*[59]

He would have been only fifteen. That is about the same age as Jesse James, who we know asked to serve with Quantrill but was refused because of his age. Bloody Bill Anderson had no such reservations and did recruit Jesse. But this calls into question Bill Cantrell's claim; it most likely was a story told by an insecure young man trying to build a reputation.

After the War

In 1867, Bill jumped on a Missouri River steamboat in St. Louis and was carried up into Dakota Territory. We have considerable information about him at this stage because he threw in with another plainsman, Joseph Henry Taylor. Taylor was a journalist who wrote extensively about his experience on the Dakota prairies and the people he lived with. Taylor and Bill worked together as wood hawks.

Missouri River Wood Yards

Gold was discovered at Alder Gulch, Montana, in 1863. The quickest way to reach these goldfields was by steamboat up the Missouri from St. Louis and through Dakota Territory. The steamers ran on firewood, and they used an impressive amount of it: "Nearly daily, the journey must be interrupted to procure fuel wood. Steamships consumed a prodigious quantity of wood, twenty-five to thirty cords every twenty-four hours."[60]

The wood yards were small businesses set up every fifty miles along the Missouri River during the days of the paddleboat steamer to satisfy this need. They will often be referenced in this story, as the horse thieves frequently made the wood yards their camps. "1867 marked the peak year of steamboat travel on the upper Missouri, when seventy steamboats and twenty-two hundred passengers journeyed to Fort Benton."[61]

Wood hawks carved a home out of the wilderness along the Missouri River, built themselves a cabin and chopped river bottom woodlands into usable logs to fuel the steamers. A ribbon forest of cottonwoods, green ash and oak lined the Missouri River as it meandered through the open plains.

Being a wood hawk was the more certain way to make money from the Montana gold rush than prospecting. In 1869, Bill Cantrell and Joe Taylor were employed at a wood yard called Tough Timber, near present-day Washburn, North Dakota, on Painted Woods Creek.

Taylor tells it this way:

> *A party of this class of men, together with some professional hunters, wolfers, and trappers, having congregated at the Painted Woods—a heavy body of timber on the Missouri, midway between the military posts of Forts Rice and Stevenson—during the autumn of 1869, a band of eleven of them were enlisted by Morris & Gluck, two enterprising wood yard proprietors, to open up a new yard between that point and Fort Stevenson. The point selected was called Tough Timber, near the present town of Hancock, McLean County.... The buildings constructed by the woodchoppers at Tough Timber consisted of two large log shacks facing each other, with a horse stable at one side between the main buildings, the whole enclosed with a picket of sharp pointed logs, placed upright. The stockade was located near the lower end of the timber among a scattering bunch of big old cottonwoods and within one hundred yards of the river.*[62]

A “WOOD-HAWK.”

Rufus Zogbaum’s sketch of an 1884 Missouri River wood hawk and camp. *Yale Collection of Western Americana, Beinecke Rare Book and Manuscript Library, Yale University.*

Work for the wood hawk was hard labor, resulting in excellent fitness. A chiseled frame was the product of such a life. Big Bill was strong, tenacious and a man of some courage and cunning.

HOW DO YOU GET A NAME LIKE FLOPPING BILL?

It was here that William Cantrell earned his sobriquet. Let's let Taylor explain as only he can. The following entry was taken from the diary of Joseph Dietrich, woodchopper, jotted down in November 1869 while at the stockaded wood yard at Tough Timber:

> *Nov 19 Friday—Weather splendid all day. Went out hunting in the afternoon with Bill, he shot a big buck deer. The fortunate slayer of the antlered buck above mentioned was a verdant appearing fellow called by his comrades Big Bill, from his oversize, being but a beardless youth of twenty winters. It was probably Bill's first trophy in the deer killing line and it was the first fresh meat brought into the cook room since the camp was organized. The big chap from Arkansas was the hero of the evening following this event....He recounted some previous experience as a wood chopper, and explained a kind of artistic move with the axe blade, which he termed "flopping." Bill's story and the droll native Arkansas twang in its recitation, put his group of listeners in gladsome mood, and Johnny Dietrich suggested that as the Indian method of bestowing proper names was the right thing, he suggested that William the slayer of the antlered buck be duly anointed and christened "Flopping Bill," which motion was acclaimed by all present, and thus was the appellation confirmed.*[63]

Feeding the riverboat steamers was summer work. It is likely that come freeze up, Bill, like most wood hawks, headed out onto the prairies to trap wolves. Wolfers shot buffalo or other large mammals and then injected strychnine into the corpse. The poison killed the wolves that would scavenge on the carcass. Their frozen bodies, left on the ground, would pile up; the trapper would collect them; and more would come. When the first steamers returned in spring, the trappers turned the wolf pelts to cash, and the work of selling chopped wood would begin again.

No one intended to stay a wood hawk or a wolfer. It was a suitable way for a young man to save some cash before moving into a more respectable career.

Bill became acquainted with all the territory up into Mouse River country in central North Dakota and all along the Missouri into central Montana. This knowledge would come in handy for his future infamous career.

Wood Hawk Conflict with Native Americans

The Missouri River forest was also an important resource to the Plains tribes. This was their winter home. They cut the tops of cottonwood trees to feed their ever-growing horse herds as emergency winter food. The wood hawks and the Native Americans were making their living from the same limited resource.[64] This competition made life hazardous for the wood hawk. In the years before 1876, the Missouri River was a war zone. The Hunkpapa Lakota, led by Sitting Bull and Chief Gall, had taken control of the territory west and south of the Missouri as it winds through North Dakota. It had been the hunting grounds of Hidatsa and the Mandan. But their friendship with the Europeans had meant constant contact with disease; by 1840, their numbers were so depleted they could no longer defend themselves against their longtime enemy, the Lakota.[65] The war between these parties was deadly and without quarter. Wood hawks placed themselves right on the front lines of the battle between the Hunkpapa, the Three Affiliated Tribes and the U.S. government. The wood hawk business made them a target, and many died.

> *The life led by these isolated wood choppers or owners of the wood yards, was, owing to the hundreds of miles of territory roamed over by bands of hostile Indians, likened unto a guard or sentinel continually at his post. His life or his property was ever insecure. Thus it was, that during the years above mentioned (1867–69), nearly or quite one third of these men so employed lost their lives, the wood destroyed and stock run off by Indians.*[66]

In fact, in 1869, the Sioux complained to the military about the Tough Timber camp at Painted Woods and were threatening to attack Cantrell, Taylor and their team. This did not transpire, but in Montana, there was an all-out war with the Sioux.

Liver-Eating Johnson was a wood hawk. In 1869, he took part in the Wood Hawk War with the Lakota in Montana. The Sioux first killed a dozen woodcutters near Fort Union. Later, Johnson and several others at their camp at the mouth of the Musselshell repulsed an attack. (George Grinnell, who will be introduced later, was in this group.) Because they were using sixteen-shot Henry rifles against the muzzle-loading trade muskets, they killed or wounded ninety Sioux. Then the wood hawks put the skulls on stakes and lined the riverbank with the gruesome sight. These were left as a warning to all others that this wood yard was not to be trifled with. The Sioux never bothered them again.

The Reeder Trial, Life in Bismarck and Berthold

Bill continued as a wood hawk near Painted Woods until about 1870, working for Charley Reeder. A métis coworker named Johnny Bucktail killed Reeder, their boss. The courts called Bill as a witness in the Reeder murder trial. He spent several months in Yankton, DT, for this.

Around 1872, Bill, though still in his early twenties, took a stab at land speculation in the rough-and-tumble railroad town of Bismarck. Speculators tried to guess where the tracks would cross the river and where the town would grow. A man named Edmund Hackett was also engaged in this endeavor. Undoubtedly, the two met. Bill missed it—they platted the city in a different area. His foray did not prove profitable, so he sought his fortune upstream.

Bill moved up the river to Berthold and worked there for a time before continuing his push farther west, as did so many other plainsmen in the 1870s, to follow the buffalo, the game and the riverboats.

The Floppin' Bill known by Joseph Henry Taylor seemed to be a man of reasonable character. No evidence of a sociopathic personality or that of a heartless killer. Yet Bill Cantrell became the coauthor of one of the deadliest chapters in Old West history.

Bill's Brush with Death

Bill worked for Durfee and Peck, who held the government contract to conduct trade with the Indians. It was during this time that he demonstrated fortitude in the face of danger. In May 1875, he and a métis man, Billy Benware, left Fort Peck, Montana, to water some cattle.[67] One cow got stuck in a mud hole, and the two of them were working to get her out. Benware did not bring a gun, and Flopping Bill had left his up on the shore. This was unfortunate because five Sioux warriors were watching them from the willows. Billy Benware noticed them first and, with no warning, took off running, grabbed Bill's gun and headed as fast as he could back to the fort. Bill, now cut off, was left with only the option to run and hide in willow brush. The five opened fire, and a bullet struck him in the groin. Lucky for Bill Cantrell, the Indians did not realize he was unarmed, and this saved his life. They were waiting him out when help came from the fort. The bullet wound laid Bill up for some weeks. The steamboat *Key West* took him to Fort Buford to be placed under the care of the fort surgeon.[68]

Musselshell Wood Yard and a Wife

Around 1878, Bill became the proprietor of a wood yard of his own along the Missouri near the Musselshell. This is the Montana Missouri River breaks country, beautiful and wild still today. Lonely Bill found a companion—an Assiniboine woman—whether they married we do not know, but they lived together there for some time, up to and beyond 1880.

Many of the plainsmen took Native women as paramours or wives. Yellowstone Kelly lived with a woman he seemed to care about but showed a prejudice that he did not equate his relationship with her as one equal to that with a white woman. Sometimes these men treated the women with respect, but sometimes the relationships were abusive.

North Dakota's first rancher, George Grinnell, married a youthful woman of mixed race—white and Hidatsa. Her parents educated her in eastern religious schools, and she was a devout Christian. She entered the relationship with chief hopes of a helpful marriage, but he came close to killing her on occasions when he was drunk—which was often. On one drunken day in 1888, he tried to run her and their baby girl down with his horse. Trying to protect herself and her child, she wrapped her hand in the decorative leather necklace around her husband's neck[69] and hung on to save her life. He fell from his horse on top of her, and she did not let go—fearing a beating. She choked him to death. The locals gave her a trial and found her not guilty. The jury of three determined Grinnell died "through an act of Almighty God by the hand of His agent Josephine Grinnell."[70]

How Bill Cantrell felt about his Assiniboine woman or about how he treated her we have no record, but it did not end well.

The Nosey Gang

The Métis and the Sioux made peace in the 1860s, and trade began between them.[71] Some Métis became a source of guns and ammunition for the hostile Sioux, which the American military was trying hard to control. But trade meant something else, too—whiskey. Not just any whiskey, but Indian whiskey. Here's the Missouri River recipe, according to Teddy Blue:

> *One-barrel Missouri river water, 2 gallons of alcohol, 2 oz. Strychnine, 3 plugs tobacco, 5 bars of soap, ½ lb. red pepper, add some sage brush to taste, then boil till brown.*[72]

These Métis, like many fur traders, took advantage of Native American vulnerability to alcohol to garner the better end of fur trade deals. In 1869, a supposed center of this trade was out of Fort Whoop-Up in Alberta, Canada. The Royal Canadian Mounted Police (RCMP) had been working their way west, establishing the rule of law, and by 1875 got Fort Whoop-Up under control.

According to Joseph Taylor's account, a man named Nosey was the leader of a gang that had headquartered out of Fort Whoop-Up. Now that the RCMP had arrived, Nosey needed a new base of operation. So, in the late 1870s, they shifted south into another lawless region, Bill's neighborhood, along the Missouri River Breaks at the Musselshell. They and other outlaws found a home among the wood yard camps and remote settlements in this wilderness area. In fact, they settled into a camp close to where Liver-Eating Johnson had lived a decade before at the mouth of the Musselshell.

The gang started out stealing horses from the Assiniboine, but soon they found fresh victims. Bill Cantrell got on the nasty side of Nosey, because unlike others in this area, he was not willing to cooperate with the outlaws.

Joseph Taylor tells the story:

> *One of the first that was tabooed by these gentry (Nosey and his gang) was Flopping Bill. He was "set-a-foot" early one summer's morning and he was compelled to take a trip to the fort for the purchase of another team—at the loss of considerable time and expense. Again he was visited by—the marauders—and again was his wood banking team missing: Thinking the horses had only strayed, this time he made a hunt for them but on his return was dismayed to find that his South Assiniboine bride did not come to greet him as was her usual way. She, too, had been stolen or coaxed*

away. Bill had heard of the proverb, that "Bad luck like crows never come singly." The imprint of strange horse hoofs sign was unmistakable and boot tracks of others had obliterated his own. Strong male that he was William Cantrell could only seat himself down on his deserted doorstep and cry. And yet—short as the time was—while he had sit down a Dr. Jekyll, he arose: a Mr. Hyde.[73]

According to Joseph Taylor, who seemed to know him well, what hatched in the heart of Flopping Bill was revenge. To steal his horses and his woman was humiliating. It ignited a hateful fire in this man. He would get his pound of flesh. As we have already established, Bill was tall, strong and a man of courage. What was born in his heart out of this hurt pride would be hate deep enough to warrant, in his mind, the killing of his enemy. Bill would rise with evil intent.

STOCK INSPECTOR / THIEF KILLER

Flopping Bill, stock detective. Sketch based on a photo in *Kaleidoscope Lives* by Joseph Taylor. *Sketch by Sarah Johannsen.*

We can only imagine what kind of murderous plots Bill rehearsed in his bed at night, but a perfect window of opportunity opened for this cunning man. Perhaps motivated to even the score, Bill took on a new profession, that of stock inspector working out of Maiden, Montana. "Thief killers" was another name given to stock inspectors in those days. Becoming a stock detective would become Bill's license to kill.[74]

Before August 1884, the stock detectives of Montana Territory were something like private investigators who worked for individual ranchers or worked as bounty hunters collecting whatever reward they could get for bringing in a criminal or returning stolen stock. They did not have any law enforcement authority from the government. In the late summer of 1884, the Montana Stockmen's Association hired many of these early freelancers and gave them some authority to make arrests.

In the fall of 1883, Bill and other stock detectives were searching along the Missouri in Dakota Territory for the Dutch Charley gang but lost them. That winter of 1883–84, Bill had the horse thief camps in the Musselshell staked out and under his watchful eye. They were too well armed for a couple of lone stock detectives to do anything about them. Bill needed an army.

A brief note in a Montana newspaper in April 1884 said a thief stole Flopping Bill Cantrell's horse. The paper added more details in the following week's edition. Bill, along with two stock detectives, was in pursuit of this horse and its thief, Broncho Billy. They cornered the miscreant, arrested him and collected the horse.

Detective Richardson complained to the newspaper reporter that Flopping Bill "weakened and did not have sand at the arrest." The paper dismissed this charge, as the other detective, Williams, would not affirm it and because Flopping Bill said in his own defense that "he has been in this country too long to be out of sand."[75]

Granville Stuart

Horse thieves like Nosey and Broncho Billy stole not only Bill's horses but also awakened a sleeping giant. If they had purloined solely from the likes of Bill and the Assiniboine, perhaps little would have come of this. They also collected stock from Granville Stuart, Andrew Fergus and other large ranchers who had considerable influence and power. When the horse thieves did this, they picked a fight they would not win.

In July 1884, the Montana Stockmen's Association organized vigilantes to go after the horse thief gangs. Flopping Bill knew which side of this fight he wanted to be on. The army he needed had fortuitously formed itself. So, as the posse gathered to clean out the rat's nest of horse thieves along the Missouri at the Musselshell, Bill made himself available. Here, Bill's natural leadership abilities for this kind of task emerged. He showed a willingness to do whatever nastiness the situation required, and he had the skills to do it. He had a mastery of the territory all along the upper Missouri where this work needed to be carried out. It is as if Bill were made for this day.

In chapter 6, we will pick up again with the Musselshell horse thief gangs, Bill Cantrell and Granville Stuart.

4

HORSE THIEVES DANCING AN AIR JIG

Cursed is he who hangs from a tree.
—Galatians 3:13

The United States of Lyncherdom

Mark Twain labeled America "The United States of Lyncherdom." The people of America had an evil disease of their collective soul at this time in history. This was the lynching era. After the Civil War, the practice of lynching became more common in the post-Reconstruction South. Most victims, but not all, were Black. White, Hispanic and Native Americans were also victims of lynchings.

> *According to the Tuskegee Institute, 4,743 people were lynched between 1882 and 1968 in the United States, including 3,446 African Americans and 1,297 whites. More than 73 percent of the lynching in the post-Civil War period occurred in the Southern states.*

Too often, when scholars and laypersons alike think about mob violence in America, they discuss racial violence below the Mason-Dixon line, but, as Pfeifer's edited collection explains, "In the last years of the nineteenth century and first years of the twentieth century, it sometimes seemed that lynchers had seized control of American life." It was a spirit that was not "confined to any section of the country."[76]

Frank McManus (child murderer), hanged by a mob on the block near the crime scene in Minneapolis in 1882. This is a postcard. *Library of Congress.*

Some of these extrajudicial killings became community events, publicized by the newspapers. Immense crowds gathered. They took photographs, and souvenir postcards were made of the victim and sold at local stores. Families would come and bring their children to watch as though the circus had come to town.

Vigilantes posted this in newspapers from Chamberlain, southern Dakota Territory:

> *July 4, 1884. The grandest attraction ever offered to the people of Southern Dakota. After the exercises of the day close, and at 7:30 PM; six notorious horse thieves will be suspended by the neck from elm trees in the grove opposite from the city of Chamberlain, Dakota. Let every man who wants to see a horse thief hang, come. Come one, come all. By the order of the Vigilante.*[77]

Many western newspapers encouraged lynching horse thieves as the proper solution, but they seldom called the act by its real name. Editors' euphemisms to describe this behavior suggest they were aware of the evil and masked its shame with these humorous phrases.

FOR EXAMPLE, HERE ARE some found in Montana and Dakota newspapers in 1884:

"A neck-tie party."
"Necktie managers."
"Dance an air jig."
"Disposed of under the jurisdiction of Judge Lynch."
"Dead as a horse thief at a Montana necktie party."
"A long rope with a short shift."
"Death by Ropium."
"Telegraph pole decoration material."
"Standing on nothing looking up at a rope."
"A journey by way of the hemp men route."
"Climbing the golden stairway from the end of a rope."

This satirical quote supposedly out of Texas reveals a sentiment shared all over the West:

> *The cowboys in Texas had a saying that it was better that 100 innocent men should be hanged than that one horse thief should go unpunished. Among the more cultivated and reverent that was believed to be culled from the Ten Commandments, and the cowboys pinned it to the pommels of their saddles. Sometimes in the speedy administration of justice the wrong man was strung up; sometimes a man was hoisted for taking his own horse, but as the victims of the mistake never complained, little was said about the errors.*[78]

There was just something about horse thieves that set people into a rage. Hanging horse thieves was believed by most the righteous thing to do. Newspaper editors were lynching's greatest promoters. You could shoot a man down in the street in some places and no one would notice, but steal his horse and you were promptly hanged for it.

Without in any way excusing vigilantism, it helps to look at this from the settlers' point of view to understand how law-abiding citizens might justify this kind of outright murder. There was little by way of law enforcement available to turn to in many of these places. Marshals were few in the territories and very much overworked. In 1884, in a stretch of over 250 miles, there was only U.S. Marshal Ayotte at Fort Buford, local sheriff Satterlund in Washburn, Sheriff McKinney in Devils Lake and Big Louie, the sheriff in Jamestown. Even when they caught criminals, the courts were lenient, and the guy was back to stealing in short order. This plague of criminals frustrated the settlers, so they formed vigilance committees or regulator teams along the Missouri east of Fort Buford, at Burlington, in the Villard area along the Mouse River and in McLean County.

The following story of the Staley family shows the effect this crime had on a farm or ranch trying to eke out an existence on the frontier. It nearly ruined the Staley family.

THE STALEY FAMILY

John C. Staley filed on his homestead a few miles south of Coal Harbor, a Missouri river town in freshly organized McLean County, DT. He erected a sod house and a sod barn, and in 1883, he brought his sizable family to their new home. That summer, he bought a team of horses and broke the prairie to make it ready for sowing in the spring of 1884.

He had just started planting his first crop when, on the night of May 6, 1884, horse thieves got clean away with all his stock. Ten horses and two mules gone, with no trace and only slight hope of retrieval. The Staleys faced ruin. John went to Bismarck, now forced to invest what little money he had left on four oxen. It was the only way to finish the spring's work and have a crop to show for three years of labor.

John sent his son Charles, then only nineteen, with four other teenage companions to hunt for the horses. They intersected the trail and tracked it one hundred miles along the Missouri River to the northwest to a place called "the Slides." Here the horse thieves turned north. The boys camped for the evening. Exploring the area, they found a newly dug grave so shallow they could see the man still wore his boots. A wooden headstone scrawled in pencil said, "The Sun Shine Down on Him." The macabre sight helped them realize the risk of their endeavor, and they headed home.[79]

The *Bismarck Tribune* reported that this same gang of horse thieves hit other farmers in the south McLean County area that spring. The *Tribune* identified the thieves as the "Jim Smith" gang. This Smith gang also stole

North Dakota homesteader family with sod house, barn and horses—like the Staleys.
Collection: 00009 Folder: 0001.000 Item: 00013 SHSND.

one hundred head of horses from the Indians at Berthold.[80] It is fortunate these farm boys did not catch up with Jim Smith.[81]

Later that summer, on a farm near Grand Forks, a settler named Ole interrupted horse thieves removing a team from a barn under the cover of darkness. The thieves threatened Ole, so he fired, and one rider of the night fell wounded off the stolen horse. The rustlers returned fire, driving Ole to dive behind a wagon. Two bullets went through his hat, one in the rim and one through the crown. Two hit the wood of the wagon in front of him. In the mêlée, the thieves lost the horses and ran off on foot, bleeding into the dark.[82] It was stories like this that made people afraid in their own homes.

At the heart of this issue is the question—is a person's right to property greater than a thief's right to life? Is a landowner justified in killing someone for stealing his property? Certainly, according to the laws in our time, a right to property does not supersede a right to life. You do not have

the right to take someone's life when they steal from you unless they pose a threat to your life. In the 1880s, attitudes seem to be different on this score. As we will see later, this seems especially to be true if the thief is a different race, ethnicity or class.

Specific examples like the Staleys' do help us understand the landowner's rage and give some insight into the murder of horse thieves by law-abiding people. This attitude was pervasive.

The Tom O'Neil Lynching

The *Bismarck Tribune*, reporting on the Staley theft, included this bit of inspiration in mid-May 1884:

> *Let the farmers and citizens generally of McLean county combine in a determined effort to put an end to horse stealing, capture a few of the infesting band, hang them on the spot and leave their remains dangling to*

a pole or tree as a specimen of the just rewards of horse thieves, who are pouncing down upon hard earned property of the farmers and there will be an abrupt end to horse-stealing in that prosperous region.[83]

I wonder if the writer realized the fine people of McLean County would do exactly that. In late May, after the Staley heist, the farmers from Coal Harbor organized a secret vigilance committee. They selected their captain—the local doctor and schoolteacher.[84] He then broke them into teams of three or four to do patrols. The group agreed that the word of the captain was law. He was to be obeyed as one would a military officer in wartime.[85]

One month later, on Saturday, June 21, 1884, one Tom O'Neil was traveling through McLean County, leading three horses on the Military Road along the Missouri back toward Bismarck.[86] The horses had brands from McLean County ranches and no bill of sale. A stage driver passed him near Berthold and felt he looked suspicious, so the coachman tipped off the local vigilantes at Coal Harbor.

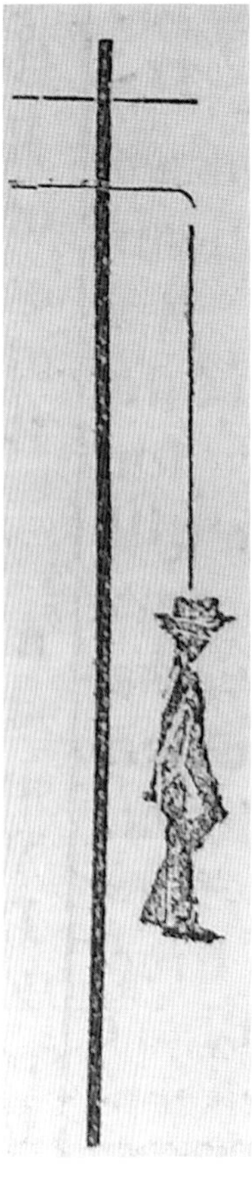

O'Neil camped at Wolf Creek. Two men located his camp and secretly watched him all night from the rushes with rifles at the ready. When O'Neil climbed out of his tent on Sunday morning, they met him at the door with "put up your hands." They took him to Jack Armstrong's sod house near Coal Harbor, where they kept him locked up that day.

The vigilance group led by the local schoolteacher/doctor held court. O'Neil's fate was under their control and debated. Being in possession of stolen horses, of course he was guilty. That settled the verdict, and so it was determined he should hang as a horse thief.

O'Neil was taken in a lumber wagon to 6-Mile Coulee, where there was an abandoned telegraph line along the Military Road. (I guess trees really were that rare in Dakota that they had to travel four miles to find something from which to hang him?) The vigilantes tied his hands and feet. They stood him up on the spring seat of the wagon now parked under the telegraph pole. One man took O'Neil's own lariat and whipped it up between the insulators and affixed the loop around his neck. Another asked if he had any last word. "You are nothing but a bunch of damn cowards" was the reply. Someone

Opposite: Engraving of Tom O'Neil as "telegraph pole decoration material." *Washburn Times*, June 27, 1884. *McLean County Museum, Washburn, North Dakota.*

Left: George Witherell, hanged from a telegraph pole in Wyoming in 1888. *Library of Congress.*

slapped the horse's rump, and the wagon lurched forward.[87] Postmaster Sam Peterson discovered the stiff, lifeless body swinging in the wind from the telegraph pole crossarm on Monday morning.

That newspaper article was prophetic. One of the vigilance patrols did capture an alleged horse thief and hang him from a pole just as the paper suggested. Peterson found the deceased with a note pinned to his shirt that said, "O'Neil the horse thief." The McLean County coroner wouldn't say, but with tongue firmly planted in cheek, the local paper determined the cause of death to be accidental or self-inflicted.[88]

Was O'Neil a horse thief? Joe Taylor did not think so. He accused this vigilance committee of hanging an innocent man. Taylor knew Tom O'Neil and claimed he spent the last year as a wolfer in White Earth River country. He claimed Jim Smith sold O'Neil the horses as a sick joke.[89] Sold stolen horses and then sent him on his merry innocent way back through the area from which the horses were stolen. I would imagine this was hilarious fun to Jim Smith, but not so for Tom O'Neil.

The farmers of McLean County were convinced that O'Neil was a horse thief. In the spring of 1884, a gang of thieves stole a team of draft horses from a settler up in the Mouse River region. Because the heavier horses slowed the gang's getaway, a vigilante posse caught up with the group and a lively shootout ensued. This posse killed one horse thief in the gun battle. They captured two others. (The newspaper believed that they hanged these two.)[90] But one got away. With no genuine evidence, the folks in McLean County assumed the one who escaped was O'Neil. According to the *Washburn Times*, this same Tom O'Neil was being hunted by the Marquis de Morès (famed founder of Medora, DT) for stealing horses in the Bad Lands. O'Neil had a reputation far and wide as a horse thief. De Morès hired Pinkertons to infiltrate gangs to identify the correct people.[91] If he thought O'Neil was a thief, maybe it was true.

So, who was correct? No one will ever know because the citizens took revenge rather than seek justice. Even if O'Neil was guilty of stealing horses, that does not excuse sidestepping the rule of law and meting out a punishment unjustly severe for the crime. Vigilante action often leads to the death of innocent people and almost always punishes people more than what is just.

The McLean County vigilance committee had other adventures. They had a good old-fashioned shootout with a gang of criminals at Stink Lake later that summer. This is only a mile outside of where the town of Turtle Lake now stands. These "criminals" turned out to be Sheriff John Satterlund's posse, returning from a foray into Dogden Butte country looking for actual horse thieves. It was all good fun. The shootout did not hurt anyone: Satterlund's big dog was winged, and another bullet blew the heel off a boot.[92] No harm, no foul.

Horse Thieves from the Way-back

The Dakota and Montana wilderness experienced a population boom after the defeat of the Lakota and their pacification in 1877. The region changed with great rapidity, especially after Sitting Bull turned himself in at Fort Buford in 1881. This rapid change left some people uncertain how to adapt and survive in the developing world that was emerging from the old. In

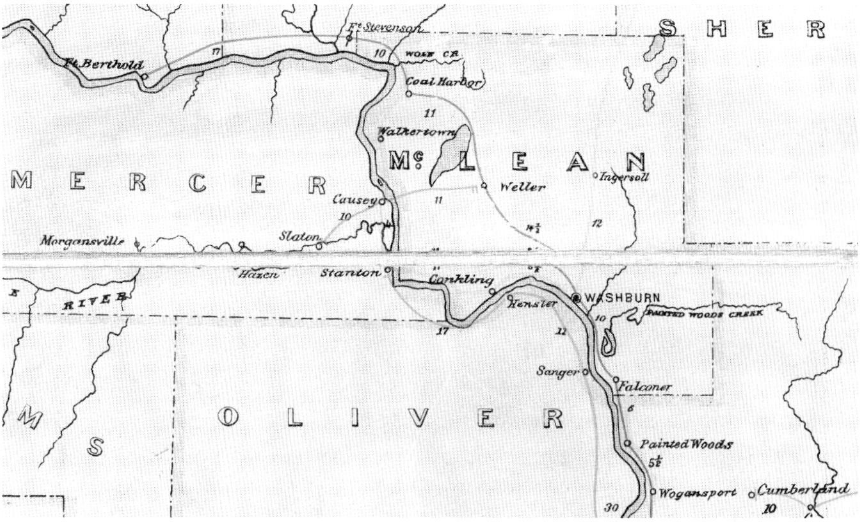

Missouri River settlements north of Bismarck in 1884. The Post Route Map of Dakota Territory 1884. *David Rumsey Map Collection, David Rumsey Map Center, Stanford Libraries.*

all the upper Missouri River country there were a few hundred—trappers, wolfers, buffalo hunters and wood hawks—who had been living off the bounty of the wilderness and now found themselves without a means of survival and not liked very much by the new residents. These were the great unwashed of the West. We can also add a few thousand Métis to this list of persona non grata. These people represented the ones remaining at the close of the fur trade era, which ended when the last buffalo herd was decimated.

The Devils Lake newspaper, in reporting Gardipee's death, referred to him as "a professional thief from Way-back, that mysterious location from whence come so many evildoers and notorious sky-scrapers."

That was the prejudged opinion about most of these original occupants of this land according to the respectable Americans from the East who were now crowding in. Anyone from the "Way-back" was thought to be a professional horse thief, an evildoer or, worst of all, a *sky-scraper*.

The American government secured all Native Americans on reservations in the northern Great Plains by 1881. But the other wild people of the West, the plainsmen and the Métis, continued as they had for the last decades: free and attempting to live off the land.

Now, homesteading intruders were flocking into what had been the Plains people's playground of abundance. These occupants from the older West

Half breed Horse Thieves of the Northwest by Frederic Remington. *Museum of Fine Arts Houston, The Hogg Brothers Collection, gift of Miss Ima Hogg. 43.34.*

had always passed back and forth over the United States–Canada border. They called it the Medicine Line. It mattered little to them. This fluidity became something of an advantage in this new dispensation. They were at home in both countries. It was a simple matter to steal a horse in the United States and drive it up to Canada to trade. Then while you are there, steal another horse and drive it back to the United States to sell it here. (The people who complained so much about horse thieves sometimes did not seem to mind purchasing a horse stolen from Canada.)

Gangs of former hunters and trappers from the "Way-back" now found a lucrative career as horse thieves, preying on the new green arrivals. They knew the backcountry and all the hidden coulees, draws and buffalo trails. They lived in two nations, which put them at an advantage against the law. In addition, stealing horses had been a way of life living with the Indians. The Indians stole from you, and if given the chance, you would steal from them. It was a plain matter to shift over and take some from their new neighbors—the farmers and ranchers filling in their country. Add to this group professional criminals like Dutch Charley and Jim Smith, who seem to provide leadership, and we are all set for the conflicts of 1883–84.

5

HORSE THIEVES AND VIGILANTES IN DAKOTA TERRITORY

Fall of '83 to the Summer of '84

Known Horse Thief Gangs

It is difficult to find detailed information about the horse thieves. They did not write books or keep journals of their work. We glean from newspapers and pioneer stories that there was a string of gangs living in camps from central Montana all the way into North Dakota along the Missouri River, then up the Mouse River and continuing to Turtle Mountain. Rough country like Dogden Butte and the sand hills of Mouse River country were staging areas for these gangs. These were suitable places to collect and hide the stolen herds before driving them to Canada for sale.

According to Joseph Taylor, these different gangs worked in concert to some extent:[93]

> *A regular line was established along the Missouri as far south as Bismarck and the run made full handed both ways. This band was not numerous but active. They established themselves at some wood yards by either buying out or running out the owner—if they could not trust him.*[94]

Here is a list of the gangs of which there is a mention in Dakota Territory in 1884. We delineate them here; you will learn more about them in the chapters to come.

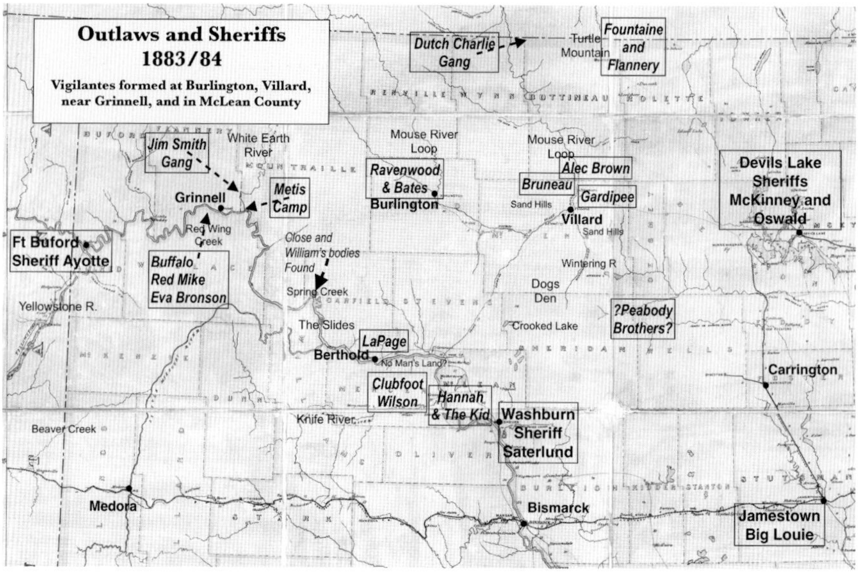

Map of outlaws, sheriffs and vigilantes, northern Dakota Territory 1883/84. Shown on the Post Route Map of Dakota Territory 1884. *David Rumsey Map Collection.*

Newspapers often accused the famous rancher Grinnell of collaborating with horse thieves. His saloon was a watering hole for all kinds of people, criminals included.[95]

The Jim Smith gang's camp was near Grinnell Landing on the White Earth River.

A Métis camp allegedly containing horse thieves was also on the White Earth River at "Outlaw Coulee."

A man named Buffalo, and another named Red Mike, came to the Missouri River in DT with stolen horses to hide in the summer of 1884. They came to escape the vigilante work in Montana that summer. They were seen at Grinnell's Landing, Nesson Flats and Red Wing Creek (Tobacco Garden). Eva Bronson was with them but likely not a thief, just a drinking buddy they picked up at Grinnell's bar or Fort Buford.

Charley "Roach" Wright (aka Dutch Charley or Charley Rhodes) and William "Club Foot" Smith had a camp in the Upper Mouse River area west of Turtle Mountain. Dutch Charley may have been the primary leader in the Mouse River area. He moved into Burlington with his small gang in the spring of 1883 but quickly passed on. His camp near the Canada border may have been the last relay station before the horses were taken into Canada. Dutch Charley was probably illiterate, so he needed a secretary. Some horse thieves used running irons to change brands. This gang forged bills of sale. James Rutherford was Dutch Charley's secretary for that purpose.[96]

Two con men, Stanley Ravenwood and John Bates, were working as part of the Dutch Charley gang (the bodies found in Crooked Lake from the introduction). They remained in Burlington, squatting on a piece of land northwest of town on the Des Lacs River. They were robbing the Burlington settlers blind in 1883 and 1884.[97]

The Peabody brothers came through Burlington late in the summer of 1884 with 150 horses they brought from Montana. They were also suspected of working with Dutch Charley and may have set up collecting horses from the Carrington, DT area.[98]

The Métis around Villard—Bruneau, Aleck Brown and Francis Gardipee very possibly—were also working with Dutch Charley. If so, at Burlington, Villard, Devils Lake and Carrington, gangs were stationed in a fan of settlements and the horses funneled north to a collection point at the border.

Most in these gangs were just petty thieves, but Wright was a truly sinister character. He supposedly committed seven murders. Many were brutal, cold-blooded and senseless. Dutch Charley Wright was hardened by years in prison and a dangerous man. The one man who truly deserved to be hanged escaped the hangings in 1884, but in 1885, he was captured by law near the Manning Ranch on Antler Creek near the border (Westhope, ND). His captors were Sheriff Conely of Miles City and a former sheriff from Jamestown known as "Big Louie" Lewis.[99]

Caribo Fountaine and Pierre Hannery worked out of the Turtle Mountain area. Hannery was captured by Sheriff Satterlund in July 1884. Fountaine was captured by the RCMP on the Canada side of the border in August 1884.[100]

A horse thief named Simpson may have been somewhere along the Missouri or Knife River.

One of the La Page brothers was hiding out in McLean County along the Missouri River.[101] There was rumored to be an outlaw camp between Fort Stevenson and Berthold. It was called "No Man's Land" (in Mercer County). Perhaps he and others used this camp.[102]

Clubfoot Wilson called Mercer County, DT, his home.[103]

Chapter 6 surveys the Montana gangs in the Musselshell country that are related to this story.

Enumerating the Death Toll of 1883–84

In the sixteen months from September 1883 into December 1884, there were over fifty violent deaths (that can be documented) related to these horse thief gangs in the Upper Missouri country in Dakota Territory and eastern Montana. Most of these are the deaths of horse thieves at the hands of vigilantes. Enumeration of this violence begins in Dakota Territory in the fall of 1883 and follows chronologically throughout north-central Dakota Territory into Montana Territory (chapter 6), ending back in Dakota Territory in the fall of 1884 (chapters 7 and 8). This book focuses on this set of vigilante killings because they are connected by the persons involved and the geography (the Upper Missouri River country) in which they occur. There were other vigilante killings at this time in eastern Montana and other parts of Dakota Territory.

The Murder of Close and Williams–Fall 1883

In the spring of 1883, the Dutch Charley gang—Wright, Smith, Rutherford, Ravenwood and Bates— left Bates Point, Montana, to escape the watchful eye of stock inspectors (see introduction). They moved through Burlington and set up a network on the Mouse River of Dakota Territory.

Stock inspectors were following the trail of this criminal gang from Montana into Dakota Territory in the fall of 1883. They lost them in an early fall blizzard.[104] Bill Cantrell was likely part of this foray. He would have been a useful addition to any manhunt along the Missouri into Dakota Territory, being so familiar with that country. Flopping Bill would again be on the trail of this gang in the fall of 1884 (chapter 8).

Our first two murders occurred in the fall of 1883 along the Missouri south of present-day Parshall. While there is no proof of who killed them, it is possible that it was Flopping Bill. Here is the story:

It was the last days of September 1883, when two wood hawks—Billie Close and Jack Williams—set out from the Close wood yard at Strawberry Island on the Missouri River (about twenty-five miles east of Fort Buford). With a wagon and a team of horses, they headed to Fort Berthold to purchase a load of corn from the Indians. Their trip should have taken a week, but they did not return when expected. Friends set out looking for them, and at first, they could not find the pair. Then an accidental grass fire exposed their bodies along the trail at Shell Creek on the western edge of what is today McLean County.[105]

One had been shot in the head—the other decapitated. Searching the area, friends found their wagon, but the team of horses was gone. A noticeable wad of bills was protruding from the pocket of one victim.[106] What kind of thief would steal the horses but have no use for the money?

The local wood hawks and ranchers jumped to the conclusion that this was the work of stock thieves. It was not long after that someone spotted, at a distance, a yoke of oxen being led away by three Métis who had stolen the pair. These culprits left an obvious trail, so the local people pulled together a small posse. Following the track, they found the oxen—now butchered, the meat stacked in piles and the ox hide stretched out over the meat. People just assumed these thieves were also responsible for the gruesome death of Close and Williams.

The posse hid at the crest of the coulee and waited all night. At daybreak, a wagon and three men appeared, coming up the coulee. Since they believed these to be murderers, they would show no mercy. When in range, the posse opened fire and killed all three, along with their team of horses. The vigilantes piled the team, the bodies of the three men and the wagon in one enormous heap and left them to decay. This was often the way, leaving the bodies unburied as a grisly warning to the imagined criminal element.[107] The vigilantes then began looking for others they suspected of criminal activity. They knew of a log cabin camp of Métis on White Earth River.

According to Lutie Breeling's book written years later, the vigilante posse then descended on this camp of Métis on "Outlaw Coulee" within earshot of Grinnell Landing and riddled it with bullets.[108] This was November 4, 1883. Fortunately for the outlaws, Lieutenant Bell from Fort Buford, with fourteen enlisted men of F Troop, Seventh Cavalry, arrived and rescued the Métis from the vigilantes. Lieutenant Bell took the Métis to Fort Buford and then escorted them into Canada and released them.[109]

It is interesting to note that Vic Smith, in his book *Champion Buffalo Hunter*, attributes the murder of Close and Williams to Flopping Bill. If Bill was with the group trailing Dutch Charley's gang along the Missouri in the fall of 1883 (as Johnson told Usher Burdick), then perhaps there is something to this. It is an odd thing that Close and Williams were carrying a combined $275 on their persons and this money was untouched by the thieves. What is the point of being a thief if not to take money? However, a posse of stock detectives might leave the money.

Why would stock detectives kill innocent people? If the Billie Close team of horses had Montana brands with no bill of sale, then yes, they might. These victims lived a short distance from the Jim Smith hideout and so it would not be surprising for them to be offered a good deal on a team of horses. Vic Smith does not explain why he thought Flopping Bill was responsible. Vic Smith is often unreliable as a source and guilty of embellishing the truth. He hated Bill so we cannot say for certain.[110] We know the military did not hold the Métis thieves at Outlaw Coulee accountable for this murder. The post report only says they were "committing depredations on settlers in the vicinity."[111]

Let's start a count of the death toll for fall 1883 through 1884 in the Upper Missouri country. We will count Close and Williams as no. 1 and no. 2. The three ox thieves follow as no. 3, no. 4 and no. 5. That a shootout occurred at Outlaw Coulee is confirmed by Fort Buford post records, so another two or three killings here are possible. Lutie Breeling's book claims some Métis were killed, but the post report does not mention this.

See Table 1 on page 95 for a list of killing in the fall of 1883, along the Missouri in Dakota Territory.

HORSE THIEF ACTIVITY FALL 1883

In the fall of 1883, a friend of Gardipee's named Frank Bruneau (paper spelling was Burno) stole a fine team of horses from none other than Edmund Hackett off his ranch at Hackett Falls. The newspaper later reports that Bruneau was never heard from again. They left us to wonder if this is because he escaped to Canada with his contraband or if Hackett and whomever he could recruit to help caught and hanged Bruneau.[112] Was he number 6? It is impossible to know.

In September 1883, the Jim Smith gang cleaned out the barns at the Weller stage station in McLean County. After the Weller raid, Sheriff Satterlund of Washburn headed out in October 1883 to White Earth country, traveling undercover hoping to infiltrate the Jim Smith gang. He hung out at Fort Buford and at Grinnell's Landing to collect intel about the gang's movements. He found that Jim Smith was an admired Robin Hood type in that area and people protected him. A resident of Weller was also in the area looking for his horses, and he blabbed a description of the Washburn sheriff to the people there, blowing Satterlund's cover. The sheriff got within a few miles of the Smith gang, but they were tipped off, and he lost them. He returned home in December empty-handed.[113]

Sheriff Satterlund said this about Jim Smith:

Horse thieves cleaned out the Weller stage stop, McLean County, DT. *Date: 1883 1889. Collection: 10158 Folder: 0003.000 Item: 00026 SHSND.*

> *The most notorious horse-thief of the whole infernal outfit appears to be a man named James Smith. The power which this man has acquired over the demoralized peasantry of the Buford country is strikingly like that singular popularity which Jesse James enjoyed in the backwoods districts of Missouri. Smith has followed the business for years, and appears to be very proud of his calling. His manners are pleasing, and he might easily be mistaken for a "perfect gentleman." When he enters a saloon, all hands are politely invited to drink with him, and such kindly attentions as these, together with his "slick" talk, have won the affections of the people entirely. "You bet," said one man to Sheriff Satterlund, not suspecting his identity, "I'd ride fifty miles any time to save Jim Smith from arrest."*[114]

FLOPPING BILL AT BATES POINT, MONTANA

In the winter of 1883–84, Flopping Bill was spying on the Bates Point camps on the Missouri at Pochette Creek, Montana, fifteen miles downstream from the Musselshell. One person called it a blacksmith shop.[115] The James Wood Yard was nearby. Bill even made a visit undercover to get the lay of the place and to gather intel regarding numbers and defenses. Working with stock detectives, he had his eye on this enclave, but he would need something of an army to root it out. Next summer it would be Granville Stuart providing the troops.[116]

THE WORK OF DAKOTA VIGILANCE COMMITTEES IN THE SUMMER OF 1884

Continuing in chronological order, in May 1884, the Jim Smith gang began again in earnest, hitting farmers and ranchers, such as the Staley family in chapter 4, in the McLean County area.[117] This was becoming a plague.

In June 1884, a gang of four stole another team of horses near Villard along the Mouse River.[118] They were driving the team toward Canada, presumably toward Dutch Charley's relay camp. A vigilante committee from Villard set out in pursuit; it is conceivable that Hackett or some who worked for him were a part of this posse. They caught up with the thieves and killed or captured three; the captured were hanged (no. 6, no. 7 and no. 8). One of these thieves escaped.

The vigilantes from Coal Harbor thought the escaped man was Tom O'Neil and hanged him on June 22, as described in chapter 4 (no. 9).[119] Sheriff Satterlund was touring the Mouse River sand hills and Dogden Butte country about this time. On his return, he had the famed shootout at Stink Lake with the McLean County vigilance committee.[120]

(Chronologically, the Montana killings would fit here, but we will visit that story in chapter 6.)

In June and July, the newspapers reported that Fort Pembina sent troops to protect the farms and ranches in Rolette and Cavalier Counties against a band of horse thieves "that are terrorizing the country by running off horses by the wholesale."[121] This was most likely the work of the gang out of Turtle Mountain.

The *Bad Lands Cowboy* reported two hundred horses stolen from the Medora area in 1884.[122] Even the Marquis de Morès lost three horses that winter. Obviously, gangs were working this area as well, but who and from where was not clear. In 1885, a posse from Medora searched for thieves along the Missouri and Knife Rivers, so it is likely it was these same gangs that would be cleaned out in 1884, as the search in 1885 did not turn up anything.[123]

ALECK BROWN

In August, things got busy again in Mouse River country. An infamous plainsman named Aleck Brown lived in a log cabin camp along the Mouse River like Gardipee's. He had gotten into stealing horses and received word a posse was coming to get him (presumably the Villard vigilantes). Brown demanded his Métis wife escape with him, but she refused. He forced his wife onto a horse and tied her hands to the saddle. The struggle spooked the horse, which bolted away, running wild, and killed the young woman. I am going to count her death as no. 10. The white vigilantes did not hang Aleck Brown; members of the Métis community did. They did not tolerate this abuse.[124] Aleck Brown is no. 11.

Gardipee's First Arrest

It was also in August that a group of Métis stole another team of horses. Francis Gardipee was with them. Why this honest mail carrier might have turned to thievery is explained in chapter 1. We assume the theft occurred somewhere near Devils Lake, since Sheriffs McKinney and Oswald of that town were pursuing the thieves. They caught up to this gang along the Mouse River before it passes into Canada. Presumably they were headed to Dutch Charley's relay station. Another shootout: the lawmen killed two (no. 12 and no. 13), and two ended up in jail in Devils Lake. One of the jailed was Francis Gardipee. It is interesting to note that Gardipee was out of jail in only one month. We wonder why? Was it because he was innocent? Perhaps he was at the wrong place at the wrong time. Or is this an example of the leniency of the courts in those days complained about so much in the papers?

We find Gardipee back home near Villard in late November. His immediate neighbors—Eugene Fish, JB Rosencranz and the Inkster family—seemed to accept him back. But returning home now, having a powerful enemy in Hackett and with the reputation of associating with horse thieves, would prove to be a severe mistake on his part.[125]

See Table 2 on page 96 for a list of killings in Dakota Territory in the summer of 1884 along the Missouri and Mouse Rivers.

Moving the Horses

These gangs seem to have created a network and cooperated to move the stock to Canada for sale. We learn in 1885 what happened to the Staley horses that had been stolen in 1884 by Jim Smith of White Earth River country (see chapter 4). A rancher, Jack Manning, saw one of the Staley horses in Canada at a "sale barn" in Moosomin in 1884. Manning's ranch was near the border at Antler Creek (near Westhope, ND). Following Manning's tip, young Charles

The Posse by Charles M. Russell. *UBP Amon Carter Museum of American Art.*

Staley, now age twenty, continued his search in the spring of 1885 and was remarkably successful. He found all their horses in Canada and returned with all but one. He was advised by the "Red Coats" (Royal Canadian Mounted Police) but did all the collecting by himself with a friend. Their horses were sold by the thieves to ranchers along that ancient trail to the Hudson Bay, which in reverse is the Road to the Mandan. Staley went up as far as 150 miles north of Brandon, Manitoba, picking up nine horses found at various remote ranches he investigated along the way. One man stubbornly refused to surrender the horse because his wife loved it. He did pay for it.[126]

Summary

In Dakota Territory, by the end of the summer of 1884, the actions of horse thieves, vigilance committees and lawmen had resulted in the death of thirteen people and possibly more along the Missouri and Mouse Rivers. Most of the people killed were Métis.

We will now jump back to the beginning of the summer of 1884 in eastern Montana and follow how this same story played out there before ultimately finishing in Dakota in October and November.

6

THE MONTANA STRANGLERS IN MONTANA

Granville Stuart is called Mr. Montana, the model of the powerful rancher in Old West novels and movies. Stuart and his Montana Stranglers wrote one of the bloodier chapters of Old West history.[127] It is a famous chapter in Montana, but few people know it ended in McLean County, North Dakota. There is a direct connection between the horse thieves at the Musselshell in Montana and those in Dakota Territory. There is also a direct connection between Gardipee's dead body found in Crooked Lake and the events set in motion by Granville Stuart in Montana in the summer of 1884.

In 1857, Granville Stuart came to what would become Montana Territory, later founding the town of Deer Lodge and operating a butcher shop catering to gold miners. Granville was first and foremost a cattleman. Stuart's initial exposure to vigilantism was at San Francisco in the 1850s and then later at Bannock, Montana, in the 1860s. At the time, these examples were deemed necessary and successful in dealing with a lawless element. This predisposed Stuart to look to vigilantism as a possible solution again in 1884.

While in Bannock, Granville Stuart made friends with people of power, wealth and influence. In 1879, he was working as a bookkeeper for his friend Samuel T. Hauser at the First National Bank in Helena, Montana. Stuart, a cattleman in Montana since 1858, could see the opportunities for cattle ranching in the wide-open range of eastern Montana, now available for settlement since Sitting Bull's Lakota and the Blackfeet were pacified. He

Left: Granville Stuart, photo by L.A. Huffman. *Montana Historical Society*.

Below: East Central Montana, key locations noted from story on George Franklin Cram's Map published by A.C. Shewey and Co., 1883. *David Rumsey Map Collection*.

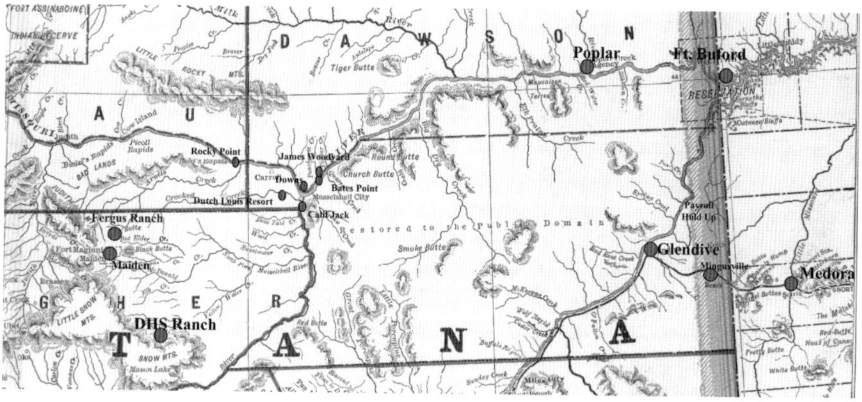

convinced Hauser and Davis to invest $150,000 in the enterprise. Stuart borrowed $20,000 from Hauser as his part. They located the eight-hundred-acre ranch on a beautiful spot south of the Judith Range near Flat Willow Creek. The group purchased 9,400 head of shorthorns from a cattleman in Montana and Oregon. In 1879, Stuart turned their herd out to wander the surrounding open range.

They called it the DHS—Davis, Hauser and Stuart Ranch. He built the ranch house near some year-round springs on Ford Creek. The life of Granville Stuart was like that of Edmund Hackett: a leader, a visionary, an articulate man well-liked and admired—often elected to public office but a complete failure in finances and in life. He died bitter and penniless.[128]

Between 1879 and 1886, the DHS operation peaked with forty thousand head of cattle spread over many miles of the open range. Initially, the partnership was successful. Many other large and small outfits filled the void left by the Native Americans and the buffalo with astonishing rapidity. In Montana and Dakota Territory, within the first few years after 1880, the region experienced a population boom in both people and cattle.

Montana Way-back

There was another class of people who lived in Montana. They were here first. Buffalo hunters, wood hawks, wolfers, trappers, and Indian traders, most had made an honest living off the bounty of the wilderness but now were falling on hard times. Many were of mixed race, the second and third generation created by the fur trade era. They lived in log cabin camps in the shrinking wilderness country. The people of the Way-back.

The last Montana buffalo disappeared in 1882. Vast areas were now hunted out of all game. Some populations starved to death because they could no longer sustain their families in the traditional fashion.[129] The railroad replaced the riverboats, so the need for wood hawks was dwindling fast. With Indians now on reservations, most Indian traders were out of business. Many of the traders, wood hawks and hunters lived in camps along the Missouri River. These camps typically comprised a log cabin or two with a teepee nearby. It was a wild badland where hunting and trapping could still produce some kind of living. This was the Missouri River breaks country up and downstream from the mouth of the Musselshell.

There was a third class of people. Professional criminals, although few, offered leadership to easily influenced people from the Way-back now struggling to survive. Many were on the run from the law in more civilized areas. These regions were nearly lawless and so a haven for sociopaths.

Otis Tye Account and the Missouri River Camps

Otis Tye was a hunter/trapper based out of Bismarck. In the fall of 1884, he was floating down the Missouri from Fort Benton back home to Bismarck. He and his friend got "froze in" at the Musselshell and spent the winter. He described the camps and the folks who lived in them. His version of this story is from someone who counted himself as one of the people from the camps. They were his friends and peers. He provided a perspective on the Montana part of this story from a North Dakotan.

Otis Tye writes:

> *The fall of 1883 I was trapping on Upper Missouri. This was a wild broken badland country. Deer were plentiful, big wolves and quite a number of Mt. Lions. My partner and I thought we had played in luck to get hung up in such a good place to winter as it was only a few miles upriver to the trading store kept by Billy Downs, an ex-Canadian mountie. He was married to an Indian woman and his father and brother lived there with him. Just below the mouth of the Musselshell River on the north side of the Missouri lived old man James and his two boys. A little farther downstream lived two Squaw men, Pete Proctor and Jim Sullivan. About four miles or so below our camp was a wood yard run by a man by the name of Bates. He had a set of blacksmith tools and his place was known as Bates Blacksmith Shop. In this wild country, a few miles was no bar to being neighborly and I soon became acquainted, as people passing up and down to the trading store would stop in and have a cup of coffee or sometimes to get a little fresh meat.…I became quite well acquainted with a number of people, Mr. Downs and family, Mr. James, Mr. Bates, Mr. Martin, Jim Orson, Henry Shannon (Cherokee), Pete Proctor, Jim Sullivan, and a number whose names I have forgotten.*

Tye mentioned meeting two other "men" introduced to him by Mr. Martin. He did not remember their names, but one turned out to be a woman dressed in men's clothing.

Farther upstream, about thirty miles from the Musselshell, there were other small towns and camps. Rocky Point was a trading post with two saloons, a few businesses and a steamboat landing, and it had a telegraph line to Fort Maginnis. These were honest establishments. But Rocky Point was also home to horse thieves Red Mike and Gallagher. Continuing upstream would bring you to the post office called Claggett at the mouth of the Judith. On Crooked Creek was a ranch run by the horse thief "Dutch" Louis Meyer.

These towns and camps were home to many regular people trying to make a living in the changing times. Melton Marsh owned the saloon in Rocky Point. He was on the Maiden stock inspector's payroll at fifty dollars per month for information about the activities of the horse thieves in his area.

Otis A. Tye (*left*) and John McKay, 1880, Bismarck, DT. *Courtesy of Curt Bigelow, descendant of Otis Tye.*

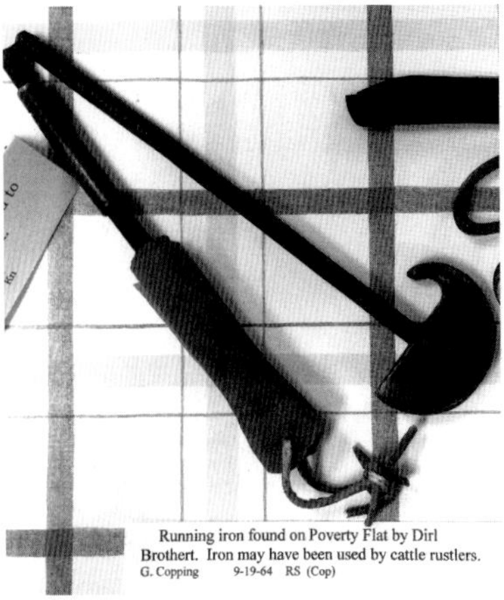

Running iron found on Poverty Flat by Dirl
Brothert. Iron may have been used by cattle rustlers.
G. Copping 9-19-64 RS (Cop)

Running iron, used to alter brands. Folds up, easily hidden in a saddle bag. *Frontier Gateway Museum, Glendive, Montana. Photo by author.*

Horse thieves and criminals also occupied these enclaves. Just as these wilderness people welcomed Otis Tye, they also welcomed others who came to live in their wilderness homes. Most were honest folks, but some were professional criminals like Dutch Charley, California Jack, Stringer Jack, Long Hair Owen and Rattlesnake Jake. They were a bad influence, recruiting hungry young men looking to make a fast buck. The camps became hideouts and staging locations for gangs of thieves. They preyed on the outfits big and small to the south like Granville Stuart and Andrew Fergus and then would bring the stolen stock here to the Missouri River Breaks. They hid the horses in the deep canyons, rebranded them and then ran them east to sell in Dakota Territory or north across the Canadian line. Most thefts were horses. Cattle were difficult to move quickly and keep hidden.

This situation became unbearable for the ranchers. In 1883 and 1884, ranchers were complaining of 3 percent losses of their stock to the rustlers.

> *Isolated ranches, continually at the mercy of the outlaws and rustlers, lived in daily fear of losing their stock and even life itself. No "nester" out of sight of his horses and cattle, could feel reasonably certain that he still possessed them. Some found it advisable to sleep in mangers of their stables, rifles in hand to protect their horses. The region was losing heart under the curse of organized hordes of outlaws, against which the established agencies of law were well-nigh powerless.*[130]

THE 1884 MONTANA DEATH TOLL BEGINS

After Jim Smith stole the Staley horses in McLean County, young Charles Staley was heading out to track him down as described in chapter 4, but his mother disapproved. Staley recalled, "My mother was a God-fearing woman, and objected to our going; saying, 'The thieves have the horses. Let them go and God will punish them.'"

Charles wanted to help God out, but his mother proved correct. This happened on Jim Smith's very next project. In May 1884, road agents—Jim Smith, Yam James, Dutchy Rolles and four others—all decked out in black slickers, attacked the military payroll wagon on the trail from Glendive to Fort Buford. Captain Whipple, expecting the attack, secretly switched the $18,000 payroll over to the ambulance wagon. A running gun battle with the payroll wagon led to the death of Sergeant Conrad and the wounding of two privates.[131] Captain Whipple escaped with the cash in the ambulance. His ruse worked. This would be the first shock to hit these western communities that spring. The outlaw element had become bold and reckless, even attacking the military. These are deaths no. 14 and no. 15, as one private died later that summer from his wounds.

A fifteen-year-old cowboy on the 101 Ranch watched this gang of unsuccessful thieves cross the Yellowstone River a mile below the ranch headquarters. One of their number had a wounded leg. The thieves, not wanting to be slowed, murdered him with a shot to the chest and left his body to lie on the west side of the river.[132] A few weeks later, the body of this outlaw was discovered by authorities. The newspapers reported his name was James Smith (no. 16).[133] Was he the same gang leader from White Earth River? Probably so—he was never mentioned in the papers again after the spring of 1884.

See Table 3 on page 96 for a list of killings in Montana in the summer of 1884, before the Stranglers were organized.

CREATION OF THE MONTANA STRANGLERS

In April 1884, the stockmen's association held a meeting in Miles City, Montana. One major item on the agenda was the growing problem of rustling. Some wanted to organize public raids on the camps of the thieves. Stuart opposed this. He had a different plan. He agreed to raids, but his idea involved working in secret. Stuart's posse of "secret" vigilantes became known as Stuart's Stranglers in the papers even before the summer ended. They are often also called the Montana Stranglers.

ROOSEVELT NOT INVOLVED

Teddy Roosevelt's biographer claimed that he and the Marquis de Morès met in Glendive, Montana, with Granville Stuart in June and asked to join this secret posse. As Hagedorn tells the story, Stuart refused to allow this because their involvement would attract too much attention.[134] This story is not true. Douglas Ellison effectively proves Hagedorn mistaken. See endnote for references that refute this widely accepted narrative.[135] Neither Roosevelt nor the marquis were in Medora more than one day at the same time in June. Such a meeting would be impossible. As we will see later, the marquis did get involved but Roosevelt did not.

FIRST LYNCHING IN MONTANA 1884

Marsh, the saloon owner at Rocky Point, wired Stuart that the thieves boasted that if the owners wanted their horses, they should come get them. The actions of the criminal gangs were becoming brazen. By July 1, 1884, there was a consensus among the ranchers that they must act. Granville Stuart took the lead and recruited Gus Adams, a professional stock inspector from Miles City. What follows in Montana is the well-known deadly summer of 1884. The secretive attacks began.

On June 25, two Métis—Narciss Laverdure and his uncle Joe Vardner from Rocky Point—stole seven horses from a sheepherder. A neighbor, William Thompson, recognized the horses and yelled to the thieves to stop. They fired at Thompson, and a running gun battle ensued. Williams captured the young Laverdure, but his uncle escaped. A posse later trapped him. He was killed in a protracted gun battle. Young Narciss (aged twenty-five years) was cussing his uncle for talking him into this. It was his first violation, but he had committed an unforgivable sin. In the early morning hours of June 27, vigilantes stole Narciss Laverdure away from his guard and hanged him. A sign was affixed to his back—"Horse Thief."[136]

The killings in May/June 1884 set the tone for the summer, as the papers of the region reported it all. These two were no. 17 and no. 18. Granville Stuart and his associates would take it from here.

MCKENZIE AND FRIEND, THE STRANGLER'S FIRST VICTIMS

Reece Anderson was Granville Stuart's closest friend. Their families lived in the same house. On July 3, 1884, Anderson and associates cornered a Scotch Métis named Sam McKenzie in a canyon. He was caught red-handed with two stolen horses. McKenzie was a well-known horse thief. According to John R. Barrows, after capture, Anderson brought McKenzie to Stuart's house and fed him supper. They often seemed to befriend their captives to put them at ease and attempt to get them to surrender information about others. When Barrows awoke the next day, McKenzie was gone. Later that day, he passed McKenzie's body hanging from a tree, publicly displayed on the road halfway to Fort Maginnis from the DHS.[137] McKenzie was killing no. 20.

The official accounts come from Granville Stuart in his book *Forty Years on the Frontier*. Another source is an article written by Oscar Mueller based on information he got from William Burnett, a vigilante himself. Burnett was a true Texas Trail cowboy and a legendary cattleman. He worked for Stuart. Burnett agreed to tell the story of the Stranglers to Mueller only when all the other players were dead. Twenty years after the events, he felt free to pass on his side of the story.[138] This should give some indication of the secrecy that surrounded the activities of the vigilantes. These two sources defend the actions of the vigilantes as necessary, given the circumstances. It would seem likely that given the acts they admitted to, there were also some things done that they did not want the public ever to know—things that were so embarrassing and damning that Burnett would not want to be revealed even after his death.

Here is a case in point. Otis Tye recorded that a man in December 1884, in Mandan, Dakota Territory, claimed to him to have been a part of these raids in Montana.[139] Tye does not give a name. But the man said that when McKenzie was captured, there was another with him. During the apprehension, the vigilantes shot and killed this person. They then discovered that the person was a woman dressed in men's clothing. Tye claimed that this was the same couple he met up on the Missouri during his stay in the camps. This may be true; it would not be surprising that Burnett or Stuart did not include this part of the story. To capture and kill McKenzie would be to everyone's approval. He was a recognized and hated horse thief. But to kill a woman in the process would have been an embarrassment.[140] According to the code of ethics these cowboys lived by, killing or harming a woman was not tolerated. In this case, they also lived by the same rules as northern Minnesota ranchers dealing with problem wolves—"Shoot, Shovel, and Shut Up." This was adverse publicity and something men who would run for political office would not want revealed. If this happened, you would expect it to be buried. She is counted as death no. 19 because it was a day before McKenzie.

Rattlesnake Jake and Long Hair Owen

On July 4, the day after McKenzie was hanged, Rattlesnake Jake and Longhair Owen picked a fight with the people of Lewistown, Montana, over a horse race. Some say these two were in partnership with McKenzie and together they were planning on a raid while the ranchers were in Lewiston for the celebration. When Jake and Owen found out what happened to McKenzie, it put them in a foul mood. They began shooting up the town; people scrambled for cover to save their lives. They killed one citizen, and an all-out gun battle ensued right in the street of the one-street town during the celebration. The townspeople riddled the two desperadoes with bullets, shooting them dead in front of the photographer's tent.[141] This was not an act of vigilantism; it was simple self-defense by the people of Lewistown. Still, these three are added to the summer's tally of violence—now at no. 21, no. 22 and no. 23—and it was only July 4.

Andrew Fergus

Andrew Fergus was a big rancher. Fergus County, Montana, is named for him. He was also a leader of the Montana Stock Association and organized his own posse to support Stuart. On July 7, he and three others headed below Rocky Point looking for Dutch Louis, who camped on Crooked Creek. Someone warned Dutch Louis, Gallagher and Red Mike, and they escaped to the Little Rockies. Stuart's book claims that Red Mike and Gallagher were hanged and only Dutch Louis escaped. Stuart was wrong. The death toll remained at twenty-three. The Fergus group stayed in this area for about a week, until July 14. Red Mike turned up later in Dakota Territory.

The First Raid on the Musselshell Camps

Stuart sent out a party of fourteen riders on July 7. William Burnett led this posse and had with him Reece Anderson, Gus Adams and Lynn Patterson and some others. Burnett's description explains why they went out and what happened:

> *A man and a boy rode into the (DHS) ranch from Pease Bottom on the Yellowstone and told Mr. Stuart he had fifty head of horses stolen*

> *and that he had trailed them to the mouth of the Musselshell on the Missouri....Granville...told me to take what men I wanted and go down and get the horses. "If you find the horses belonging to this man which have been stolen, use your own judgment in dealing with the thieves and I will be back of anything you do." We went in on them at daylight one morning. They had a lookout scouting around (California Jack); he saw us about the time we saw him and he rode to give the alarm. A boy named Lynn Patterson and myself was on good horses so we headed him off, told him to unbuckle and drop his arms on the ground—I noticed he was riding a Pioneer Cattle Company horse. The four other men were in the cabin asleep. The horses were in the corral. Their brands had been burned out but the man and boy said that they was their horses—they should have known because they had driven them all the way up from Nevada. They took them and was well pleased.*[142]

This gang of vigilantes broke in on the four sleeping in the cabin and dispatched them with their pistols. California Jack was one of the professional criminals with a $10,000 bounty on his head. Gus Adams, the stock detective, wanted to turn him in for the reward, but Burnett would take no chances he might go unpunished. They hanged him from a stout limb of a cottonwood tree. Such was the culture of the Texas cowboys who had brought in the herds on the Great Western Trail. It was only July 7, and the total dead from the summer of 1884 had jumped up five to twenty-eight. This was still just getting started.[143]

See Table 4 on page 97 for a list of those killed in Montana by Stuart's Stranglers in the summer of 1884.

Billy Downs Trading Post

Across the Missouri River from this camp, at the mouth of the Musselshell, was the trading post of Billy Downs. Reece Anderson, with a few of the vigilante party, visited the Downs establishment on about July 9. They found cattle hides and dried beef in storage. They pointed out the stolen horses in his corral. Billy said he gained them by trade, and that if stolen, they could take them. The vigilantes took the horses but returned in the evening and asked Billy and a man with him named Charley Owens to accompany them. They declined, but Anderson insisted. They hanged Billy from the pommel of his saddle and dragged him until dead, as a suitable tree was not handy.[144] Charley Owens was also killed that day. The count was now thirty dead.

After this, the posse returned to the DHS. Both Stuart and Burnett criticized Reece Anderson concerning this action. Their opinion was that yes, Downs had received stolen horses, but he did not deserve to hang. Anderson could not join in on the next adventure. This was his only consequence for the murder of Billy Downs and Charley Owens.

Cantrell Leads the Stranglers to the James Wood Yard

As the group was returning to the ranch, William Cantrell caught up with them and provided helpful information. This is the William Cantrell introduced as Flopping Bill in chapter 3. Flopping Bill had been working with stock detectives since the fall of 1883. He had been spying on the James wood yard all winter in 1884.[145]

Flopping Bill knew of an outfit near Bates Point, twenty miles downriver from the Musselshell. This was the James Wood Yard run by the old man and his two adult sons—Sam and Yam.[146] Bill said they had about one hundred stolen horses and that he did not approve of thievery and offered his services. Granville Stuart gave immediate orders to go after them.[147]

The name of the leader was Stringer Jack, a professional criminal.[148] Yam James may have been a part of the gang that attacked the military payroll in May with Jim Smith. This gang was dangerous, and arresting them would not end in any other way than in their death. That is why Cantrell did not do this himself. Cantrell had plenty of sand, but he never took a chance of losing. The numbers were always strongly in his favor whenever he made a move to apprehend a criminal. This was the group he was after, but he knew he needed numbers to get them.

Stuart sent word to the Fergus team, and they joined up with Stuart's gang and together headed toward the James Wood Yard on July 15. The place comprised a rough log cabin with portholes and a tent some distance away. A typical setup for these camps. They held the horses in a corral attached to the cabin. It was river bottom with cottonwoods, thickets and grassy meadows.

Scouts first approached on July 17 and patterned the actions of the guards. The rest of the party arrived on the evening of the nineteenth. They surrounded the place after dark. The details of almost every account

Rufus Zogbaum sketch of the Montana Stranglers at James Wood Yard after the fight. Stuart is in the middle with his back showing. *Yale Collection of Western Americana, Beinecke Rare Book and Manuscript Library, Yale University.*

of what happened next is different. Exactly what happened cannot be ascertained with certainty.

The vigilantes opened fire on the tent first, wounding some inside. They then moved their attention to the cabin, which allowed five in the tent to slip out through the brush and escape down the river on a makeshift raft. We know that Stringer Jack, old man James and his two sons were killed in the shooting. The cabin was set afire, which killed another one to three. These six bring our death toll to thirty-six.[149]

On July 23, Stuart and others took the retrieved horses back to the DHS and returned them to their rightful owners. Stuart then went to Helena to attend the stock association convention. He placed Flopping Bill in charge. From then on, Cantrell took over as the leader of the Stranglers, under Stuart's authority, but Stuart was no longer a direct participant. The Montana Stockmen's Association elected Stuart as president of the organization, tacit approval of the actions of the Stranglers.

Stuart reported to the officers at Fort Maginnis that fugitives were coming downriver on a raft. The fort relayed this information by telegraph to Poplar, Montana. The military there began searching for the wounded escapees.

Zogbaum's Report

Rufus F. Zogbaum, a reporter and artist for *Harper's Weekly*, was passing in a steamboat when all this transpired. He saw Billy Downs's widow come screaming to the boat only hours after Billy's hanging. Farther downstream, he saw the smoke rising from the James Wood Yard. Stuart's gang came on board to get water and supplies. Billy Downs's brother was on the boat, and on hearing the news, he locked himself in a cabin, back to the wall, guns loaded. He was kept safe only because the passengers kept his secret. As the steamer continued downstream, it reached the fort at Poplar, Montana. Indian scouts from the fort had located the escaped fugitives. They were hiding in a willow jungle along the river and were relieved to be apprehended by the soldiers of Fort Poplar and not the Stranglers. Zogbaum observed all of this and sketched it.[150]

THE CAPTIVES.

Rufus Zogbaum sketch of the captives at Poplar River. *Yale Collection of Western Americana, Beinecke Rare Book and Manuscript Library, Yale University.*

Capture of Escapees

Reece Anderson and other DHS riders were deputized and sent to pick up the captured thieves. (According to the Fergus diary, Cantrell and Adams were not present.) Here the story gets fuzzy; on their return with the captives, "someone" intercepted them while they camped on the Musselshell near its mouth. This party took the captives and hanged them, lined up in a row on a log that ran between two log houses at Bates Point. The captives' names were Johnnie Owens, Swift Bill, Sy Nicherson, Phelps and Eugene "Dixie" Burr. Dixie Burr was Granville Stuart's nephew and the son of Fred Burr, who was Stuart's close friend. The death toll now stood at forty-one.

The Old Recluse

Joe Taylor and Vic Smith recounted a story of an old hermit. It may be another of the embarrassing incidents that Stuart and Burnett would like forgotten. The old man was an innocent recluse living along the river in a log house filled with books. Innocent, with one exception: he owned a horse with a DHS brand and no bill of sale. He had purchased the horse from some cowboys, he said. They asked him if he had any last words. As he had none, they threw a rope over a tree branch, and he was hanged.[151] The count was now forty-two. See Table 5 on page 98.

Cherokee's Observations

Otis Tye said he ran into his old friend Cherokee (Henry Shannon) in 1885.[152] He and Tye lived together in the camps in the Missouri River Breaks. Cherokee (an admitted horse thief himself) claimed to have been watching from the woods while the James Wood Yard fight unfolded. He followed a group of the vigilantes along the Missouri River. Cherokee also claimed they captured someone he referred to only as Dick. Dick was not at the wood yard fight, but a vigilante posse killed him later when he returned to the site to look for money he knew was hidden there.

Cherokee also related the story of the McLaughlin place. This was another of the camps along the river where the vigilantes worked. It is also another embarrassing story that we would not expect the vigilantes to tell. Cherokee told Tye that McLaughlin *was starting a little place; he didn't belong to an outfit but was an old cowpuncher, a two-gun man and they knew it, so they were not going to take any chances and as they rode up and a man opened the door, they opened fire, killing him and the baby he was holding. But as it so happened, it was not McLaughlin. It was another man who was helping Mrs. McLaughlin as the baby was sick.*

Cherokee gave an estimate of those killed in the camps along the Missouri: "I don't know how many were wiped out but of what I know of the camps there must have been about 30."[153]

SUMMARY

The count we have for the fall of 1883 up into the summer of 1884 is now at forty-five. Those killed by Stuart's Stranglers, if we add in the embarrassing ones and what Cherokee reported, number twenty-four (including McKenzie and friend). The evidence for some of these is questionable, so if we count only those Stuart and Mueller admit to, then the count is nineteen. At the end of his article, Mueller writes, "Summing up the facts, the DHS raids were responsible for the death of a minimum of 15 men and a maximum of 18." I assume he does not want to give credit to the Stuart gang for the five who escaped in the boat, but that is naïve. Stuart added one more at Long Point than Mueller.

Everything covered in this chapter so far is well known and explored by many authors and historians (except for the Otis Tye material). What happened next is at best only given a passing mention as a part of the Montana Strangler story. For most, that story ended on August 1, when Granville Stuart stepped out of the picture. There was a string of dead bodies spread all over North Dakota that begs to differ. The Montana Stranglers' killing did not end until late November and early December on and around Dogden Butte and in McLean County, Dakota Territory.

THERE WERE FIFTY-FOUR KILLINGS with excellent to fair historical support in the fall of 1883 to December 1884. Of these, twenty-two were in Dakota Territory, thirty-two in Montana Territory.

Factual Certainty*

1. This is a well-established fact supported by several sources. (36)
2. This is highly likely true but only reported in the newspapers, no body found or other corroborating evidence. (11)
3. These are believable stories that come from good sources but only one source. (5)
4. These are stories told many years after the fact that cannot be substantiated with other sources. (3)
5. This is the Bruneau account, newspaper only says he was never heard from again. We do not know what this means. (1)

Also, we are not sure what happened at Outlaw Coulee. Lottie Breeling claims people were killed; Fort Buford Post records do not support this.

Table 1. Killing in the Fall of 1883, Most along the Missouri in Dakota Territory

#	Date	Name of Person Killed	Location	Killer	Factual*
1	9/83	Close	Shell Creek	Flopping Bill?...	1
2	9/83	Williams	" "	...or unknown	1
3	10/83	Métis ox thieves	Near Missouri Mountrail County	MO River Vigilantes	3
4	10/83	" "	" "	" "	3
5	10/83	" "	" "	" "	3
?	11/4/83	Métis Camp on White Earth River DT	Outlaw Coulee White Earth River	" "	5
?	Fall	Bruneau	Mouse River near Canada?	Hackett?	5

TABLE 2. KILLING IN THE SUMMER OF 1884 IN DAKOTA TERRITORY ALONG THE MISSOURI AND MOUSE RIVERS

#	Date	Name of Person Killed	Location	Killer	Factual*
6	6/84	Métis horse thieves?	North of Villard	Vigilantes from Villard?	2
7	" "	" "	" "	" "	2
8	" "	" "	" "	" "	2
9	6/22/84	Tom O'Neil	Coal Harbor, McLean Co.	Coal Harbor Vigilantes	1
10/11	8/84	Aleck Brown and his wife	Mouse River	Brown and other Métis	1
12	" "	Métis with Gardipee	Turtle Mountain	Devils Lake Sheriff	2
13	" "	" "	" "	" "	2

TABLE 3. THOSE KILLED IN THE SUMMER OF 1884, BEFORE STUART'S STRANGLERS WERE ORGANIZED

#	Date	Name of Person Killed	Location	Killer	Factual*
14	5/12/84	Sergeant Conrad	North of Glendive	Jim Smith et al.	1
15	" "	Private (died from wounds in June)	" "	" "	1
16	5/13/84	Jim Smith	" "	Fellow thieves	1
17	6/?/84	Joe Vardner	Rocky Point, MT	Thompson et al.	1

18	" "	Narciss Larverdure	" "	Rocky Pt. vigilantes	1
19	7/2/84	Woman in men's clothing	Fort Maginnis	Anderson, Burnette et al.	1
20	7/3/84	Sam McKenzie	" "	" "	3
21	7/4/84	Rattlesnake Jake	Lewistown, MT	Citizens of Lewistown	1
22	" "	Long Hair Owen	" "	" "	1
23	" "	Citizen of Lewistown	" "	Jake and Owen	1

Table 4. Those Indisputably Killed by Stuart's Stranglers in Montana in the Summer of 1884

#	Date	Name of Person Killed	Location	Killer	Factual*
24	7/7/84	California Jack	Musselshell River	Stuart et al.	1
25	" "	Unnamed horse thief in cabin	" "	" "	1
26	" "	" "	" "	" "	1
27	" "	" "	" "	" "	1
28	" "	" "	" "	" "	1
29	7/9?/84	Billy Downs	Mouth of Musselshell	Anderson et al.	1
30	" "	Charley Owens	" "	" "	1
31	7/20/84	Old Man James	Long Point	Stuart/ Flopping Bill et al.	1
32	" "	Sam James	" "	" "	2
33	" "	Yam James	" "	" "	2

#	Date	Name of Person Killed	Location	Killer	Factual*
34	" "	Stringer Jack	" "	" "	1
35	" "	2? Unnamed horse thieves burn in house	" "	" "	1
36	" "	Uncertain who burned in house	" "	" "	2
37	7/25?/84	Sy Nicherson	Hanged at Bates Pt.	" "	1
38	" "	Dixie Burr (métis)	" "	Rumored to have survived	3
39	" "	Phelps	" "	?	1
40	" "	Owens	" "	?	1
41	" "	Swift Bill	" "	?	1

TABLE 5. THOSE INCLUDED IN THE OTIS TYE AND JOSEPH TAYLOR ACCOUNTS

#	Date	Name of Person Killed	Location	Killer	Factual*
42	7/12?	The Old Recluse	Missouri	Flopping Bill	3
43	7/25?	Dick who returned to wood yard	James wood yard	?	3
44	Late July	The man…	McLaughlin Ranch	?	4
45	" "	…and the baby at McLaughlin's	" "	?	4

Table 6. Those Killed or Captured by Montana Stranglers in Dakota Territory in Fall of 1884

#	Date	Name of Person	Location	Killer	Factual*
	~10-11-84	?	Bad Lands	Terrorized by Flopping Bill	?
	10-12-84	Two Shields	Bad Lands near VI	Fake hanging by Flopping Bill	2
46	10-18-84	Buffalo	Near Nesson Landing	Flopping Bill and 16 Stranglers	1
47	" "	Evan Bronson	" "	" "	1
	" "	Red Mike	" "	Tortured and released	1
48	~10-30-84	Simpson	Missouri River?	" "	2
49	" "	Sixteen-year-old	?	Flopping Bill and Stranglers?	4
50	~11-12-84	Skeleton (a Peabody?)	East of Dogden Butte	Flopping Bill and Stranglers?	2
51	11-16-84	Stanley Ravenwood	Hangman's Pt. Crooked Lake	Flopping Bill and 16 Stranglers	1
52	" "	John Bates	" "	" "	1
53	" "	Francis Gardipee (Metis)	" "	" "	1
	~11-20-84	Club Foot Wilson	Victoria area	Released	1

#	Date	Name of Person	Location	Killer	Factual*
	" "	Two String Hannah	North of Bismarck	" "	1
	" "	The Kid	" "	Returned to Jail	1
54	11-26-84	La Page	Berthold	Flopping Bill and 16 Stranglers	2

7

THE MONTANA STRANGLERS IN DAKOTA TERRITORY, PART 1

Through the Bad Lands to the Missouri River

By August 1, 1884, Stuart's vigilantes had finished their deadly work in Montana. The DHS apologist accounts leave this as the end of the story. Oscar Mueller writes at the conclusion of his article:

> *Summing up the facts, the DHS raids were responsible for the death of a minimum of 15 men, with a maximum of 18, during 1884. They had no part in the killing of the two desperadoes at Lewistown, or the Breeds at or near the mouth of the Judith River, or in the raids conducted in other parts of Montana or Dakota. The movement of Central Montana ended with the hanging of the captured thieves about August 1, 1884. From then on, the Stock Inspectors took over the job of enforcing the laws, and peace descended upon the range in Central Montana.*[154]

Now, while it may be true that Granville Stuart no longer had direct involvement, the story of the Montana Stranglers did not end with him. Flopping Bill continued this work as an official stock inspector in August, carrying forward the mandate given to clean out nests of horse thieves. It continued as brutal and violent as ever, but now they carried their efforts into Dakota Territory.

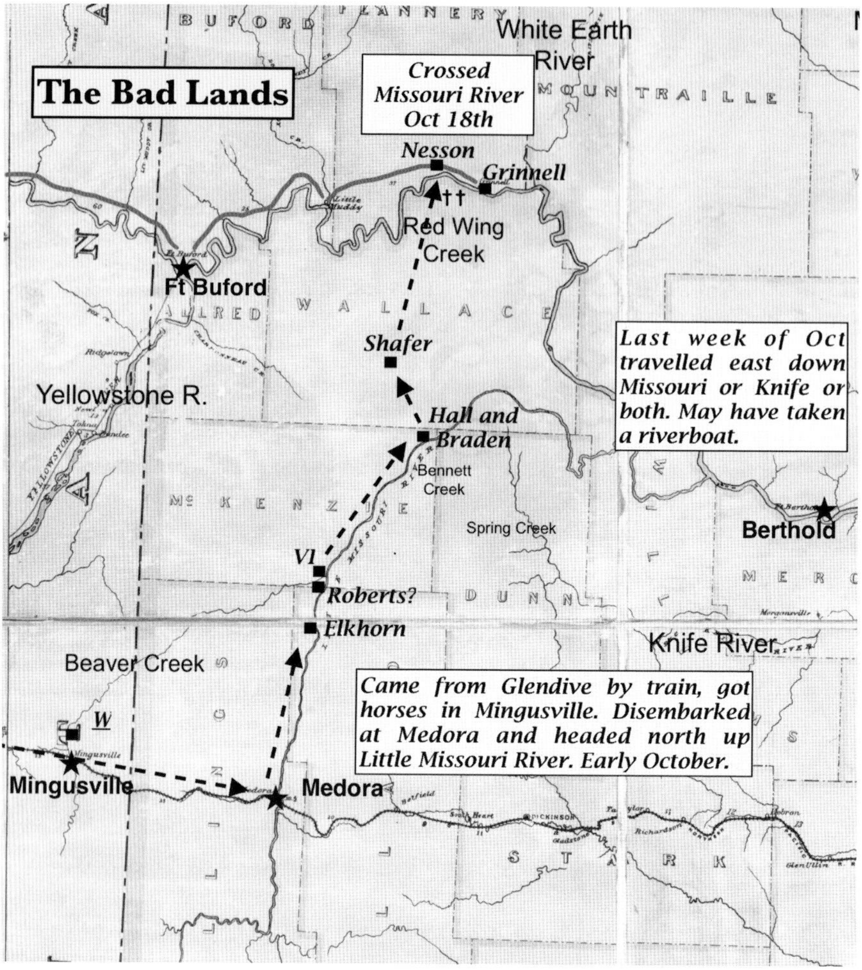

The Montana Stranglers path of terrorism through the Bad Lands in October 1884. Shown on the Post Route Map of Dakota Territory 1884. *David Rumsey Map Collection.*

September Trip to Little Rockies

In September, William Cantrell led a group up into the Little Rockies of Montana. His mission was to capture Dutch Louis Meyer, who escaped in July from the Andrew Fergus posse. The miners and ranchers in that country were not helpful to the vigilantes. They warned and protected Dutch Louis, and again he escaped.[155] This shows that if a community cared, they could prevent the bloodshed. But as we will see, some would invite the violence and use it to strengthen their own interests.

OCTOBER IN DAKOTA TERRITORY

Bill Cantrell launched a new horse thief hunting expedition into Dakota Territory, starting out early in October 1884.[156] Flopping Bill was now a stock detective representing the Eastern Montana Stockmen's Association. In the years after these events, Granville Stuart referred to Flopping Bill as "our stock detective."[157] A newspaper quoted Bill on his return to Montana in January 1885 after the foray into Dakota, stating his mission: "He was employed by the Eastern Montana Stock Association to recover stock and arrest horse thieves."[158]

Cantrell organized and led this trip but as a hired stock detective under the authority of the Montana Stockmen's Association.[159] Why would the Montana Stockmen's Association send a team deep into Dakota Territory? How did Cantrell make this decision? Was he invited? Did he have intelligence about horse thieves operating in Dakota Territory? Did he come to apprehend suspects who escaped from Montana? There are reasons to believe all of this to be true. The vigilantes would capture or kill several horse thieves in Dakota Territory in possession of Montana horses. They also apprehended escaped convicts.

The Marquis de Morès invited the Montana Stranglers to the Little Missouri River valley. *Collection: 00042 Folder: 0002.000 Item: 00079 SHSND.*

MARQUIS DE MORÈS CONNECTION

The Marquis de Morès and Pierre Wibaux were large ranchers in the Bad Lands and leading members of the Little Missouri Stockmen's group, which was a subsidiary of the Eastern Montana Stockmen's Association. Over two hundred horses were stolen from the Bad Lands area in 1884. In February 1884, the marquis had several ponies stolen. It should come as no surprise that he and Wibaux would ask for help from the stock detectives.[160] It was clearly these two who invited the Montana Stranglers into the Little Missouri valley.

John Goodall, who worked for the Marquis de Morès, claimed he drove a herd of horses from the Marquis Ranch at Medora to the Wibaux Ranch near Mingusville, Montana, to supply this posse.[161] He was contacted by Elf Cole from Powder River, Montana, who represented the stockmen's association. Cole requested fifteen good horses, and he said he wanted the best horse for "the boss." This was a white horse called Snowball later seen at Shafer Springs and at Fort Buford when the Stranglers passed through those places.[162]

Gaining Intel

Cantrell's posse needed a guide. They had the wonderful fortune of gaining the coerced help of Louis La Pache. He was under the custody of U.S. Marshal Ayotte stationed out of Fort Buford.[163] La Pache was a Métis horse thief from Dakota Territory and familiar with the gangs and hideouts along the upper Missouri. His help may be why they were so effective.

> *La Pache had been for some years a horse thief in the upper country. He had concluded to reform and promised a United States marshal that he would retire to his farm in Canada and be honest; he started on foot, but after becoming weary he saw a horse and saddle in a convenient place, his old weakness returned, and Mr. La Pache started the road to reformation. He was overtaken, and now is in the Custer County jail.*[164]

This seems to be one of the stock detective's modes of operation. Capture a horse thief, make him feel that if he gave information and cooperated, he would be treated with leniency. So, La Pache, regardless of whether he liked it, was now their informant.

The Stranglers in Dakota

Supposedly, the stockmen's association paid each of the Stranglers $35 to $50 per month. It was said that "they were shifters, irresponsible parties, men without character or property, ex-convicts and horse thieves."[165] There are records of five names in this posse that entered Dakota in October. Three are certain: Flopping Bill Cantrell, Louis La Pache and a Mr. Stuart (no relation to Granville). The Berrys at Mouse River reported a leader's name as Mr. Stuart, who said he was from the Box L Ranch in Montana.[166] JL Stuart was a part of Stuart's Stranglers in the Musselshell raids. His ranch was one of the twelve in the Cone Butte and Moccasin

Range roundup.[167] It seems reasonable to assume that some others from the Montana action in July were now present as well. The fourth and fifth members were a Mr. Savage and his son who later claimed they were part of this group.[168] The most reliable records from contemporary eyewitnesses and newspapers report the size of Flopping Bill's posse to be from fifteen to eighteen riders.[169]

The record of the workings of the Stranglers in Dakota Territory is close to complete once we piece together all the separate stories from the various sources. There are problems, though; some sources contradict one another. Each source is aware of what happened in their area, but all show ignorance of the other parts of the story. Claims are made that cannot be substantiated. Some of these accounts were passed on many decades after the fact and likely embellished. Many times, the source is based on hearsay. So, it must be acknowledged that we cannot be sure all that has been told is factual. We are certain about some aspects and fuzzy about others.

The vigilantes were secretive about their work. Only one record of a Montana Strangler admitting to his deeds in Dakota Territory was found. This one was by Mr. Savage, confessing guilt about the killing of a teenager.[170] Most took their experiences to their graves. The Stranglers did not attempt to benefit by selling their story in the years to come, as many others did with their Old West experiences. Perhaps as time passed, they were not proud of what they did. They may also have been afraid of the consequences if the

Medora, Dakota Territory, 1885. *TRC PH 1 560.14 017 (olvwork420909), Houghton Library, Harvard University.*

Office of the *Bad Lands Cowboy* newspaper, Medora, Dakota Territory, with editor Packard and his wife. *TRC PH 1 560.14 079 (olvwork421186), Houghton Library, Harvard University.*

truth got out. Vic Smith, a Dakota plainsman and cowboy, boasted in his book *Champion Buffalo Hunter*:

> *Smith immediately sent word to Bill Quantrill that for that cold-blooded murder, he would kill him on sight, unless Bill was the quickest on the draw.*[171] [Which murder is meant was not clear. In Vic Smith's autobiography, he refers to himself in the third person.]

The Strangler Train to Medora

Fifteen years after the events, a reputable source, Charlie Krug,[172] who worked for the Northern Pacific, claimed the railroad provided the Stranglers with an engine, a coach and two boxcars for their horses. This train started out at Billings and then moved down the tracks to Miles City and then Glendive, picking up Cantrell's posse. They stopped at Mingusville, Montana, to pick up horses and then disembarked at Medora, DT.[173] It was rumored they would stop at various places along the track to hunt down horse thieves and then continue, but likely this only occurred at Medora.

The *Bad Lands Cowboy*, Medora's newspaper, reported in October 1884 that the Montana Stranglers had struck in the Bad Lands. This caused considerable talk, and all kinds of rumors were afloat.[174] The word must have spread throughout the local ranches, because they rarely found anyone at home. We don't know exactly when the posse arrived at Medora, but it must have been in early October. Here they organized themselves and began their ride downstream along the Little Missouri River on its west side, heading north toward the Missouri River (See map on page 102).

They were riding through the North Dakota Bad Lands. Vic Smith gave this description of what this territory was like in 1884 (when Roosevelt moved into the area):

> *Elk were very numerous in the badlands, also mountain sheep, black-tail and white-tail deer, and bear. Antelope by the thousands wintered in the badlands breaks for shelter, and all in all it was a paradise for game. Burning veins of coal were all over the hills, and the country was covered with petrified wood....It was to this section that Theodore Roosevelt came.*[175]

The North Dakota Bad Lands today. The Stranglers followed the Little Missouri River on the far bank. *Photo by author.*

Roosevelt Connection

Every Old West Dakota story hopes for a Roosevelt connection. We have already established that he did not seek to join the Stranglers, as is often reported. We do know the Stranglers passed by Roosevelt's Elkhorn Ranch. Cantrell's posse followed the Little Missouri north into Dakota Territory in early October. That trail brought them within sight of the Elkhorn. Teddy Roosevelt left Medora for New York on October 7, but his ranch managers Sewall and Dow were keeping watch at the cabin.[176]

A few weeks earlier, Teddy Roosevelt heard that Paddock, the Marquis de Morès's foreman, boasted he would run Roosevelt off the Elkhorn. This is a piece of evidence that the marquis wanted to keep nester ranchers out of his area. Roosevelt was squatting on land the marquis had unsuccessfully used for sheep. Paddock was a Medora cowboy reputed to be an outlaw and a tough character. He had killed and he could be dangerous. In typical Roosevelt style, the future president fearlessly went straight to Paddock to confront him about these claims. When face to face with the stern young Roosevelt, Paddock folded and denied saying any such thing.[177]

Sewall's diary records a curious encounter on October 12:

> *One Sunday morning I was writing home and Dow had gone out for a walk. Suddenly I heard a great fusillade; something over twenty guns were fired as fast as I could count. Very soon afterward a half-dozen men rode up to the shack. They were cowboys. I knew one of them as the right-hand man of the Marquis de Mores and decided that they had come down to look us over.*[178]

It turned out not to be much of a threat. Paddock and the other cowboys stayed for lunch—Sewall was cooking beans, and Paddock loved Sewall's baked beans. They showed no hostility to the Elkhorn.

But what was the shooting all about? Is it possible that Paddock and his five cowboys ran into Flopping Bill's posse of sixteen, who were about that time moving up the Little Missouri from Medora? If Cantrell was invited by the marquis, Paddock and the cowboys would not be persons on his list. But perhaps he did not initially recognize them. Twenty shots in rapid succession would suggest an exchange of gunfire. If each man shot once, that is over twenty rounds. Was this Cantrell's first encounter in Dakota Territory? This is a wild conjecture but also too intriguing a possibility to ignore.

Paddock and the other cowboys who worked for the Marquis de Morès. *TRC PH 1 560.14 097b (olvwork468751), Houghton Library, Harvard University.*

The George Shafer Account

The record of the Montana Stranglers in the Dakota Bad Lands from Medora to Shafer Springs (Watford City) comes primarily from one source: the recollections of George Shafer recorded in the *Dickenson Press* on October 2, 1915, published thirty-one years after the fact. He did not observe any of this; he was born in 1888. Shafer does not list his sources; likely they are stories he heard from his father, other ranchers and local cowboys. His account is the oral tradition passed on from the Bad Lands community. One article in the *Bad Lands Cowboy* on October 30, 1884, and the few stories told by others complement and support Shafer's account. (George Shafer later became governor of North Dakota.)

See Table 6 on page 99, Those Killed or Captured by Montana Stranglers in Dakota Territory in Fall of 1884.

BEAVER CREEK

The first stop in Shafer's account was a scant distance beyond the Elkhorn Ranch at the confluence of Beaver Creek and the Little Missouri.[179] Cantrell's posse was riding on the west side of the river. They entered a ranch owned by Wm (Win?) Roberts, George Medlock and Jim Monroe. I can find no other record of these persons. There was a Win Roberts in the area. In 1885, he was arrested for stealing six horses from the Hashknife and sentenced to the penitentiary.[180] So perhaps these men already had a reputation. It is likely they were a small "nester" outfit and so not listed in any records.

Only their hired hand, the Englishman Thomas Webb, was at home. Cantrell's cowboys threw a rope around the poor man's neck and cinched it tight. They said they would spare him if he left the country and never came back. Thomas Webb was not seen in the region again. The vigilantes marked the door of the cabin with a skull and crossbones and a warning that they planned to return.[181]

CHASING OUT NESTERS

The behavior of this group sent out by the Eastern Montana Stockmen's Association was strange. According to their stated mission, they came into Dakota Territory to retrieve Montana horses and the thieves who stole them. That was not the focus of their work along the Little Missouri. Here, they were harassing small ranchers. "Nesters," they were called. Even Roosevelt did not have title to his land in 1884. He was a squatter, as were almost all others.[182] You could not register your land until surveyors did their work. So, people squatted on the un-surveyed land and waited.

In four quick years, the cattle range was filling up. Many people were moving herds of cattle everywhere, and they were fast exceeding the carrying capacity of the land, overgrazing the prairie—a classic example of the "tragedy of the commons." Cattlemen hauled thousands of carloads by train from the east. Texas cowboys brought up tens of thousands of cattle along the Great Western Trail. They were also herded in from Oregon and other points west. By 1886, the upper plains supported 650,000 head of stock. The overcrowding was not an idle worry. Teddy Roosevelt expressed this himself.

The day of reckoning came in 1886. It was a drought year; the cattle stripped the range of grass and were going into winter in poor condition.

Above: BT Ranch, a "nester" ranch in the Bad Lands of Dakota Territory 1887. *Charles Bregler's Thomas Eakins Collection, purchased with the partial support of the Pew Memorial Trust. 1985.68.2.1074 Pennsylvania Academy of Fine Arts.*

Left: Cowboy by ranch house. *Charles Bregler's Thomas Eakins Collection, purchased with the partial support of the Pew Memorial Trust. 1985.68.2.1092 Pennsylvania Academy of Fine Arts.*

The ranchers hoped for a mild one, but what followed was the severest of winters. This one was made worse by Krakatoa's eruption in Indonesia.[183] That winter, 90 percent of the Wyoming/Montana/Dakota range cattle died of starvation and blizzards. In 1884, the large-scale ranchers could see this disaster coming. Some of them wanted to stop the small nesters from bringing in more cattle onto what would become a crowded rangeland.

Flopping Bill did not find, capture or hang any horse thieves in his ride up the Little Missouri. He did not retrieve any stolen horses. Their apologists deny it,[184] but in this area, his only actions were terroristic threats to discourage and run off the nesters. There is reason to believe that if the marquis had provided this group with resources, then they had come to the Little Missouri country at his invite. It is interesting that they did not kill anyone in the Bad Lands. From what we know of the marquis, there might be reason to expect that he had warned them not to. But he also had reason to ask them to run off the nesters and put fear in potential horse thieves.

W Bar Ranch

The next stop was at an outpost of Pierre Wibaux's W Bar Ranch on Beaver Creek in Dakota Territory. Although the headquarters of the W Bar was near Mingusville (Wibaux), Montana, most of this ranch was in Dakota Territory. Here they expected to find sympathy for their cause, as the owner, Pierre Wibaux, was a member of the Montana Stockmen's Association and helped supply the Stranglers with horses from the marquis.[185] But the ranch foreman Charley Armstrong and his associate Sid Tarbell[186] did not condone the practices of Cantrell's posse. They refused to give them any help and ordered the cowboys to leave the ranch. At least, that must have been the story they told later. While invited by the large ranchers, the Stranglers were not popular among the average citizen, so I doubt anyone would admit they assisted them.

Eaton Brothers VI Ranch

The vigilantes hit the Eaton brothers' VI (Vee Eye) Ranch, which was also on Beaver Creek, ten miles north of Roosevelt's Elkhorn.[187] Shafer said no one was home, but we have a story passed down from one old-time Bad Lands cowboy to his son, Harry Roberts. According to the senior Roberts, the vigilantes came riding into the VI ranch yard. They were all well armed and greatly intimidated this twenty-year-old cowboy. They got his horse out of the barn. The brand and markings were carefully checked, and then they looked at other stock through the corrals and the barns. When finished, a vigilante said, "I guess you are not the man we are looking for." They then got on their horses and rode away. The vigilantes left him with a spooky feeling. The experience frightened the young Roberts. He was keenly aware of what would have happened to him if a brand was amiss. He had observed suspicious transactions on a couple of occasions at this ranch. Horses were dropped off or picked up from the ranch by strangers. The whole experience was too close a call, so he quit that job and moved to another, safer ranch.[188]

According to Shafer, these vigilantes captured a Hidatsa Indian named Two Shields who had a hunting camp in the woods near the VI. They performed a mock hanging. Two Shields had a rope around his neck, the other end thrown over a tree, pulled tight, and he was dropped. The rope was rigged so as not to harm him when they let go. This was a sheer terror for Two Shields and some kind of sick amusement for the vigilantes. He was commanded to go to his cabin, stay for three days and then leave the country. Two Shields, being absolutely mortified, did exactly that. He sat on the roof of his cabin, singing and crying for three days, and then left, never to return.

A Sheep Ranch

George Shafer claims the vigilantes visited a sheep ranch run by Thomas McGregory, Scotty Dunorout and Bennett. Its location is unknown, perhaps on Bennett Creek. This is another group of names that could not be traced, another of the small nester ranches squatting on un-surveyed land. Somehow, these owners were also forewarned and so were not home. The vigilantes left the sign of the skull and crossbones on their door.[189]

Hall and Braden at Squaw Creek

Downstream, continuing to the north, they came to where Hall and Braden were running a sheep ranch on Squaw Creek. This later became the famous Long X Ranch and is now in the Theodore Roosevelt National Park North

Unit. The only person present was a hired hand, Charley Nacy. The posse burned five hundred tons of hay, the barn, their machinery, harness and all the other property; they also set the prairie on fire. Nacy was taken by force to act as their guide. The vigilantes thought he could show them the whereabouts of persons they were seeking. They held him as far as Spring Creek, where he misdirected them and made his escape. The *Bad Lands Cowboy* supports Shafer's account of this story with an article on October 30, 1884.[190] It is no coincidence that soon after Hall and Braden sold out to the Long X, a big outfit that came up the Great Western Trail all the way from Texas.

SHAFER RANCH

The Stranglers made their way up Cherry Creek and came to a spot near present-day Watford City. Charles Shafer (father of George Shafer) had built a hunting cabin at this location in 1883 and in 1884 had brought in a few head of cattle to start one of the first ranches in that area. Three cowboys— Frank Chase, Jap Holts and Kid Edgar—were in the cabin at the time the posse of riders arrived.[191] Unlike everyone else, these men were unaware of who they were dealing with or what they were there to do, so they invited the group in for dinner. After dinner, the vigilantes imprisoned the three young cowboys and told them they were about to hang from the lone cottonwood tree out in the yard. Frank Chase, articulate and clever, talked his way out of their predicament. He assured the posse he hoped to become a large rancher himself and was in complete sympathy with what they were trying to do. Chase promised he would help them any way he could. He took them out on the surrounding range to see herds of stock he claimed were his own and the big plans he had for this country. Thinking they found an ally, they let Chase and the other two cowboys go. Years afterward, Kid Edgar said, "I was never so dead sure of anything in my life as that we would be hanged to that cottonwood tree, but Chase lied out of it!"[192] It sounds as though the death toll would have jumped to forty-eight if it had not been for the silver tongue of Frank Chase.

An observation: when in the area near to the Marquis de Morès's land holdings, the Stranglers were harassing folk but not killing. Probably the marquis had invited them to help eliminate competition, but he did not want anyone murdered. Now eighty miles from the marquis, the threat of killing and actual killing began.

The First Raid on Grinnell Landing

If they entered Dakota Territory around October 10, it might take about a week to work up the Little Missouri and hit the first series of ranches. It is at this point that a Montana paper records a report that came out of Poplar River, Montana, and establishes a specific date and a location.

According to the *River Press*, out of Fort Benton, Montana, the vigilantes crossed the Missouri east of Fort Buford, coming up from the south.[193] Saturday, October 18, is the date given. If we connect this to the Shafer story, we might assume this occurred right after the visit to the Shafer Ranch. They may have come up from the Little Missouri following Cherry Creek. From there, Tobacco Garden is the most likely location of the crossing, but the article did not say. The article did say that after crossing the Missouri, they headed downriver to Grinnell Landing.

George Grinnell

George Grinnell was introduced in chapter 3 and mentioned elsewhere. After service in the cavalry during the Civil War, Grinnell drifted west through Minnesota and on into Montana. He was in Alder Gulch in the 1860s gold rush but came back along the Missouri and put down roots about 1868. Grinnell started with a wood yard and then raised cattle to sell to Fort Buford. In fact, historians credit him with being the first rancher of the northern Dakota Territory.[194] He soon added a trading post and a saloon at the landing. This was another of the log cabin camps that sprung up in the Dakota and Montana wilderness before the boom. His clientele were the people from the Way-back: Métis, trappers, buffalo hunters, wood hawks and, yes, horse thieves. His saloon became a watering hole for outlaws, Jim Smith most famous among them.

For this reason, Grinnell's place was in the crosshairs of Flopping Bill's vigilantes. Some claimed Bill and Grinnell had a falling out years before over buffalo hides and that this was a vendetta visit.[195] Grinnell had a widespread reputation of being in league with outlaws. No one claimed he was breaking the law himself, but he was trading with, supplying and protecting horse thieves and other ne'er-do-wells. We have seen how with Billy Downs, that was reason enough for his hanging. Once again, Grinnell, like the others, seemed to know that the Stranglers were coming. Early on the same day

Three Bad Lands cowboys. *Charles Bregler's Thomas Eakins Collection, purchased with the partial support of the Pew Memorial Trust. 1985.68.2.1098 Pennsylvania Academy of Fine Arts.*

the posse arrived at Grinnell Landing, Grinnell had taken the fastest route possible to the protection of Fort Buford.

It would be at this time that we would expect the Stranglers to locate the camp of Jim Smith on the White Earth River. There is no mention of him after the reported killing of a Jim Smith in May 1884 as part of the military pay wagon heist.

Bronson and Buffalo

First blood was drawn in Dakota Territory when Flopping Bill came to the river crossing at what is today called Tobacco Garden Creek. At that time, this creek on the Missouri south side was known as Red Wing Creek. Nesson Flats was on the north side of the river. At Red Wing Creek, they stumbled into a group of three hunters: Red Mike, Eva (or Eddie) Bronson and a guy just dubbed "Buffalo."[196] Red Mike and Buffalo had escaped here to avoid capture back in July around the Musselshell. These two were sure enough horse thieves. They were caught with several stolen horses in their possession.

Buffalo attempted to escape from the vigilantes but was pursued on horseback, run down and shot dead. He was buried on the spot. The sources from the day all seem to agree this was the correct thing to do with him—no tears shed. But hunting with him that day was a man of only nineteen years named Eva Bronson. He was the son of a former officer from Fort Buford—Major Bronson. The major had transferred back east a few years before, but his son stayed to adopt the life of a plainsman and hung out with the likes of Buffalo and Red Mike as his mentors. He seemed to have a drinking problem by some reports. Young Bronson, found in the presence of a horse thief with stolen horses, was judged guilty by association and hanged. Most seem to think he stole nothing but was just hunting with these guys. The killing of Eva Bronson was looked on by the people of that day as the murder of an innocent young man.[197]

A year later, Major Bronson wrote to an acquaintance who lived along the river at the Little Muddy—Bob Mathews—inquiring into the whereabouts of his son. Mathews had to break the news of this tragic death, and the major wrote back, wondering if this extreme measure was called for. Mathews told him they caught the group with several stolen horses. Young Bronson had made friends with the wrong crowd. The implication from Mathews's letter was that being associated with horse thieves was enough to justify his killing.[198]

THE TORTURE OF RED MIKE

The vigilantes, having just snuffed out two other human beings in the sight of Red Mike, certainly must have had his attention. It was time to extract information for their next pinch. They tied him to a wooden chair and built a fire under it.[199] As the flames rose, Bill grilled Mike about the whereabouts of other horse thieves. Mike kept his mouth shut. Most likely, he wished he had something to tell them. They released him to authorities at Fort Buford scorched but unharmed.[200] It is difficult sometimes to understand what reasoning this group followed. So much of it seems arbitrary. They were so quick to murder some but let others go. If

Men on horses. *TRC PH 1 560.14 093 (olvwork422584), Houghton Library, Harvard University.*

Buffalo and Bronson possessed stolen horses, how did that not make Mike deserving the same punishment?

We will add to the death toll from where it left off in Montana, with the actions from the fall of 1884 in Dakota. It begins with these—Buffalo was no. 46 and Eva Bronson no. 47. Red Mike caught a break.[201]

It should be noted at this point that it is not possible to determine the exact order of events. We have evidence by combining five sources that the Stranglers worked their way up the Little Missouri and on October 18 crossed over the Missouri to hit Grinnell's Landing. It is most logical to assume that this is the time they killed Buffalo and Bronson. It is the most likely scenario because it is on the way. But in what order did they visit the various small ranchers along the Little Missouri? The details of George Shafer's order of events, recorded thirty years after the fact, are confusing. He also seems to assume the Stranglers headed back to Montana after the Shafer Ranch. We know this is incorrect. All sources related to this story have information for their own locale but know nothing of what happened in the other counties.

See Table 4 on page 97, Those Indisputably Killed by Stuart's Stranglers in Montana in the Summer of 1884.

8

THE MONTANA STRANGLERS IN DAKOTA TERRITORY, PART 2

Mouse River and Back Home

Crossing the Missouri

George Shafer surmised the Stranglers boarded a steamboat and went home to Montana, but this is not true. He was unaware of their doings on the Mouse River. It would be more likely they caught a steamboat to Fort Stevenson. In 1884, the fort was closed, but a small community still existed there.[202] Few boats would still run in late October. If they were on a boat, it was heading downstream ahead of freeze up.

The story of the Stranglers goes silent for a few days. We have no specific reports of their whereabouts for the last days of October. They might have explored down the Knife River.[203] They showed up on the Mouse River about October 31 or November 1. Their likely path to Mouse River would be down the Knife and/or the Missouri to Fort Stevenson. From there, follow the Totten Trail to Strawberry Lake and take the road that goes to the northeast off the Totten Trail to connect with the trail that followed the Mouse River.

Seventy-Five Horses and Simpson

When they appeared at Mouse River, the Stranglers were driving in a herd of seventy-five horses.[204] From whom did they take these horses? What happened to the horse thief? This is a piece of evidence that would suggest

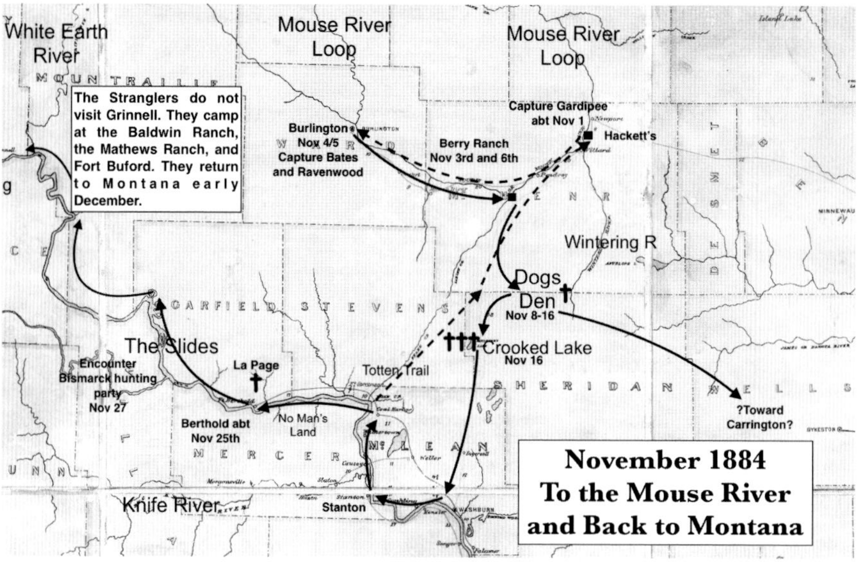

The Montana Stranglers along the Mouse River and in McLean County, November 1884. Shown on the Post Route Map of Dakota Territory 1884. *David Rumsey Map Collection.*

there are things about the activities of the Stranglers in Dakota Territory that we do not know. They had come up the Little Missouri, raiding Grinnell Landing and Tobacco Garden Creek on the Missouri about October 18. Next, we know they showed up at the Mouse River about November 1.

They collected a few horses from Buffalo and Red Mike, but it is likely they left these at Fort Buford, since they would have had to return that way. The Devils Lake newspaper reported that these vigilantes killed a man named Simpson. That is all we know about that part of the story.[205] To find seventy-five stolen horses probably meant somebody died. The sources give us only one suggestion—Mr. Simpson, whoever he was. These horses and Simpson had to have been from along the Missouri or Knife River between Grinnell's and Fort Stevenson.

Years later, Mr. Savage, one of the Stranglers, expressed remorse about a sixteen-year-old they captured. He argued for leniency, but the group, including his own teenage son, voted to hang the youth, and they did.[206] We do not know who this was, where they were or exactly when it happened, but we will add these two deaths to the tally. The man Simpson was no. 48 and the unnamed teen no. 49.

Hackett's House

On about October 31 or November 1, the vigilantes appeared at Souris City at the home of the new self-appointed County Commissioner Ed Hackett.[207] They camped on his property that night. This was Hackett's account, as recorded in the *Devils Lake Inter-Ocean* on November 22, 1884:

> *Mr. Edmund Hackett, one of the commissioners of McHenry County, has been in the city (Devils Lake) during the week. He called our attention to an item in a Bismarck paper in reference to the hanging of horse thieves in the Mouse river region.*[208] *He says the Montana Cattlemen's association have hanged at least 50 men in the past eight months. A week ago last Friday sixteen cowboys belonging to this association arrived at Souris City, on the Mouse river, and took dinner at Mr. Hackett's place. They had but little to say, but Mr. Hackett says they had blood in their eyes. The next day one Gardupee* [sic], *who lived near Souris City, was missing.*
>
> *Mr. Hackett says horse stealing has been a profitable business in the Mouse and Missouri river region the past year, but he is of the opinion that the profession will gradually fall into disrepute as the visits of the cowboys become more frequent.*

Is this number of fifty given by Hackett accurate? In this article, he is clearly reporting things he heard from the Stranglers, claims they made to him while they stayed at his home· We know of only about twenty-four they had killed by this time. It is not unlikely that there were others but probably not that many. This was probably an exaggeration.

People should not be accused falsely, even if it is done 140 years later. However, it seems a convenient coincidence that the Stranglers showed up at Hackett's place and then carried off a neighbor—whose land Hackett was trying to acquire—the very next day. Another from the Mouse River Métis community, Bruneau, stole a team of Hackett's horses one year before. One might like revenge for that. Soon Hackett would be in court with Caroline Gardipee in a land dispute. On November 6, Eugene Fish submitted a legal complaint about Hackett. Fish and the Gardipees were in the same argument with Hackett over land ownership (see ¼ of Section 31 Newport Township). Hackett had shown his disdain for the Métis people (refer to newspaper article on page 43), and we have a sense of his general lack of character.

Why did the Stranglers come to Mouse River country all the way from Montana? We know they were looking for Dutch Charley and the others in the fall of 1883. But it also appears that they may have been invited by Commissioner Edmund Hackett to get help with a nuisance neighbor. Hackett and Cantrell lived in the small town of Bismarck together, back in the early 1870s. They must have known each other. They did not catch Gardipee with stolen horses like others they executed. This was different. This was an abduction. I don't believe the cowboys would have done this without someone in authority giving them permission. The day after the Stranglers broke bread with Hackett, our friend Francis Gardipee disappeared, and he never returned.

The Capture of Francis Gardipee

Eyewitnesses report that, on leaving Hackett's home, the vigilantes explored the six miles along the Mouse River up to Newport. There they stopped at the ranch of John Rosencranz and inspected his horses. They asked Mrs. Rosencranz if they could buy some flour, as no one else would give them any.[209] This may have been because people were afraid of them and wanted nothing to do with their deadly work. It may also have been because flour was scarce and required a sixty-mile trip to Devils Lake to replace it.

Imagine the terror they would instill each time they entered a homestead and began searching through the stock. Are you sure you know that every horse you purchased had a clean title? Even Jim Johnson, a community pillar, admitted he had purchased horses from Dutch Charley Wright. Likely many people owned stolen horses without knowing it.[210]

From John Rosencranz's place, they worked their way back downstream looking for Gardipee.[211] One has to admire the effectiveness of Bill and his Montana cowboys. Sheriff Satterlund of Washburn complained about how difficult it was to capture horse thieves. In contrast, this group consistently found and captured their man within a day or two. I would think their reputation instilled fear, which would lead to intimidation that produced informants. It is likely someone ratted out Gardipee, probably to save their own neck.

We gain details of Gardipee's capture from John Inkster and James B. Rosencranz (John's brother). They described a normal gathering of friends and shock at seeing Gardipee hauled away. Surprisingly, John Inkster claimed the posse seemed to know Gardipee. Maybe it was La Pache, their informant, who most likely would have known him.

The George Inkster ranch, the Eugene Fish ranch and Gardipee's camp were all in proximity on the Mouse River. Hackett's place was also not far. Gardipee was not in his own cabin that day but rather with Eugene Fish. Others were there: six-year-old John Inkster and his mother, Fish's brother-in-law James B. Rosencranz, another Métis named Red Dog and perhaps more. John Inkster remembered they had all eaten together at his mother's house.[212] According to JB Rosencranz, when the posse rode up, Gardipee was outside, a short distance from the Fish ranch house. The cowboys caught him by surprise. Fish was in his house with JB Rosencranz. The cowboys shouted their accusation that Gardipee was a horse thief and ordered him to surrender and come with them. Gardipee froze, but Fish was ready to fight it out. He waved for Gardipee to make a run for the house. Rosencranz said they had the guns and ammo, and Fish had the resolve to shoot it out from the house in defense of their neighbor. Gardipee, though, was too afraid to run, afraid they would gun him down. Justifiably afraid. Or maybe he simply didn't want to see his friends hurt, and so he surrendered. In so doing, a much deadlier event was avoided. As he was being taken away, he yelled back to Fish and Rosencranz to tell his wife he would not be back for some time.[213]

Mrs. Inkster followed the posse all the way to their camp at Hackett's house on foot. She pleaded for Gardipee's life, but they ignored her. Early the next morning, the vigilantes packed up and Gardipee disappeared with the cowboys.[214]

Ravenwood and Bates

Their next recorded appearance was near future Velva, North Dakota, on the Mouse River on November 3, 1884. The group asked permission to spend the night in the barn at the Tom Berry Ranch.[215] On the following day, they traveled the thirty miles upstream to Burlington, DT. The first settlers had moved into that area and established the town of Burlington only one year earlier, in 1883. Many others were following. (Minot, North Dakota, would spring up twelve miles from here in 1886.)

Stanley Ravenwood and John Bates had been a part of the criminal element in the Musselshell country. They and Charley Wright came east with a herd of horses with mixed brands from Montana in the summer of

1883. Wright left soon after, but Ravenwood and Bates stayed. The pair settled in, along with the very first folks at Burlington, Dakota Territory. They presented themselves as "railroad contractors," here to sell horses when the railroad arrived. They were model citizens, even joining the Burlington Regulators organized to protect the locals from horse thieves and claim jumpers.[216]

Dutch Charley, Bill "Clubfoot" Smith, Ravenwood, Bates and the Peabody brothers were likely part of the network of gangs working with the James family in Montana, Jim Smith on the White Earth River and the Métis with Gardipee on the Mouse and up in Turtle Mountain. Not partners exactly, but they helped move horses among this loose network of like-minded thieves.[217]

Usher Burdick collected the remembrances of many Dakota pioneers. One of those was a Danish immigrant named Jim Johnson. Burdick recorded Johnson's story in the booklet *Jim Johnson Pioneer: A Brief History of the Mouse River Loop Country*. Johnson was one of the first settlers to come to Burlington in the spring of 1883. This is his version of the story. He begins with a description of Ravenwood and Bates:

> *Jim Johnson observed that the front of their wagon would be of one kind of make and the back would be of another make; the harnesses were made of rawhide, and in a conversation with them Johnson remarked, "You fellows look more like horse thieves than railroad contractors." They never manifested a very friendly feeling for Jim. The men stayed in the community, joined the Regulators and were accepted as good citizens, though Johnson never at any time was convinced that they were anything else than horse thieves. Occasionally some neighbor would lose a horse, and the Regulators, including Bates and Ravenwood, would scour the country for miles around but no trace of the missing horse would be found.*
>
> *A man by the name of Benson was running a whiskey still north of Burlington, and the contractors ran quite a large bill with him for the products of his still. On one occasion Benson dunned the contractors for some money on account, and a few nights later Benson missed some of his horses. In a day or two the contractors paid Benson cash on account which Benson was glad to accept, not knowing that the cash came from the sale of his own horses. Occasionally one of the contractors would volunteer to go in search of stolen horses for a reward, and invariably the horses would be returned and the reward paid. The contractors became popular in the community for the citizens pointed to the aid they had given the community*

This would have been the scene at Burlington when the Stranglers arrived on November 4, 1884. *Photo by LA Huffman. Montana Historical Society.*

> *in recovering stolen horses. Johnson, however, was still suspicious and thought in his own mind, that the contractors were the real thieves and had a place somewhere to the north where they assembled these horses.*

This was the situation in the Mouse River Valley at Burlington when the vigilantes arrived there on the evening of November 4, 1884. They camped in the grassy meadow just down a way from Jim Johnson's home with their herd of seventy-five horses. That night, they secretly investigated the brands on the horses in Johnson's barn while he slept.[218]

Jim Johnson's account continues:

> *Later events showed that the Vigilantes had trailed Ravenwood and Bates the fall before, but during a severe snowstorm, had to abandon the trail, convinced, however, that the thieves were somewhere along the Mouse River. They had now taken up the trail again. Bates and Ravenwood were still*

> *there, but the Vigilantes needed evidence, which at the time they did not have. While this gang was summary in its movements, yet it had some elements of a judicial body. Evidence was necessary. The next morning, after their arrival, one of their number, a Frenchman by the name of Gardipe* [sic], *got in touch with Ravenwood, who had a bunch of horses down the river. The horses were looked over, but none of them suited the Frenchman. At this point Ravenwood was asked if he had any more horses. After some negotiation, Ravenwood rounded up another bunch of horses and showed them to the prospective buyer.*

The Stranglers, with Gardipee in their possession, put him to good use and sent him to talk to Ravenwood. It seems likely they knew each other. This transaction was probably conducted in Michif, the mixed language of the Métis, and not French. To Ravenwood, this was one of his own kind wanting to buy stolen horses—discussions that must have happened many times with other Métis. I can't imagine it possible that Ravenwood did not know Gardipee.

Johnson continues:

> *Among them were several stolen Montana horses. Ravenwood was immediately held at the point of a gun, placed in irons and brought back to the camp of the stranglers. Bates was still at large, and at the time was staying with Benson, the man who ran the whiskey still. A detail was ordered to the place, and upon seeing the approach of the horsemen, Bates remarked to Benson and another who was present—Bondholder, that he didn't like the looks of that outfit. With this statement he ran to the barn, saddled his horse and was just emerging from the barn when he was met with the command "Stick 'em up, stranger," and Bates found himself confronted with several drawn pistols. Upon arriving at the Benson place, two members of the posse forced Benson and Bondholder on a woodpile with hands high in the air, while the others surrounded the barn. Bates was thus trapped before he could make his get-a-way and was immediately placed in irons and taken to camp, where he was kept under guard with his partner, Ravenwood. The two "contractors" were now in the custody of the Vigilantes and their true character was revealed. The people of Burlington, with the exception of the doubting Johnson, were very much surprised. The "contractors" owed Colton a bill for groceries and they were taken to the store in irons and told to settle their affairs as best they could. They were further told that they were soon to leave Burlington, never to return.*

"Stick 'em up." Bad Lands cowboy, 1887. *Charles Bregler's Thomas Eakins Collection, purchased with the partial support of the Pew Memorial Trust. 1985.68.2.1076 Pennsylvania Academy of Fine Arts.*

> *The stolen horses were rounded up, and on the third day after the arrival of the Vigilantes, they moved out of the valley, taking with them their two prisoners and stolen horses.*

On November 6, Flopping Bill's posse of vigilantes turned up at the Berry Ranch again, this time with Ravenwood and Bates in tow. Also, according to Belle Berry, Francis Gardipee was one of their prisoners, also in irons. The Berrys' recounted Gardipee showed some courage in the face of this trial—mostly expressing concern for his wife.

Belle Berry recalled the events with detail. The leader of the three horse thieves was a big man—this was probably Bates, who other sources say had size 12 boots. She described him as 6' 3" and well-muscled. She said he would often boast: "I kin knock a steer off his feet with one biff. Then he would swing a vicious right in the air, landing nowhere."

He was not so brave this day. The giant man drooped in the saddle, leaned and whispered to Tom Berry, "God, Mr. Berry, save me. Don't let

A ranch along the Mouse River in the 1880s. *Collection: 10147 Folder: 0007.000 Item: 00003 SHSND.*

them take me away!" He sobbed such that his Adam's apple "chased up and down in his throat."[219]

Ravenwood was a tougher-looking character, small, wiry, with catlike movements. She said he had a "glaring eye" and rarely shaved. He always had a bulge in his cheek from a plug of tobacco.[220]

Last Ride on the Ancient Road

This would be Gardipee's final ride down the Road to the Mandan. When they turned south from the Mouse River heading to Dogden Butte, they would pass one last time the place of Métis victory at the Battle of the Grand Coteau. What was once a place of miraculous intervention and glory would make Gardipee feel even deeper his sense of powerlessness. Mixed with his grief were the satisfying memories that would flood back here.

As his horse trotted along, his mind might have wandered to recall that slow jog the Métis hunting brigades would experience as they drew near a buffalo herd. The cows would be lazily grazing and then notice the approaching army of hunters. The buffalo would at first walk away, slowly picking up their pace, and when the Métis were one hundred yards out, they would bolt into a full gallop and the chase was on. These very hills surrounding Dogsden were where they ran the buffalo late summer every year, all the years of Gardipee's youth and into adulthood.

It might have been right here that Gardipee shot his first buffalo at age twelve, as most Métis boys did. With a muzzle-loading trade musket in one hand, a mouthful of lead balls and a hand full of powder, the riders plunged into the thunderous cloud of chaos. Riding alongside the beasts at full speed, at point-blank range, the hunter emptied his gun right behind the shoulder and the cow would tumble. Powder from the hand was shaken down the barrel, its end pressed to the rider's lips. He spit in a ball, primed the pan and only a minute later was ready to fire again. This adrenaline-laced excitement addicted the hunters to their work. He must have felt the disappointment of the withdrawal from that life. He missed it so deeply. It was a free, fun, exciting world they lived in for three generations. And now it would end like this.

As Maison du Chien (Dogs Den) came into sight, he felt a deep dread. He was once the terror of this mountain. His people ruled here and prospered here.[221] Now it appeared dark and foreboding. A demonic place with evil portent.

A WEEK AT DOGSDEN

The Stranglers stayed in the Dogden Butte area from November 9 to Sunday the 16.[222] People thought of it as a staging area for horse thieves and so perhaps the cowboys were using it in the same way the Yanktonai Dakota did—as a lookout to set up an ambush on anyone moving horses through the area. You can see for many miles in all directions from the top of these hills.

According to one account, the Stranglers sent a small team to search south toward Carrington. The Peabody brothers were rumored to be raiding the farms and ranches of that area.[223] This may have paid off for the Stranglers. In 1889, Jim Johnson of Burlington was riding two miles on the east side of Dogden Butte and stumbled upon the skeleton of a man still in his saddle on the bones of a horse sunken into the prairie grass. In Johnson's opinion, based on the condition of the body, this was the work of the Montana Stranglers in 1884. We will count this nameless cowboy as victim no. 50.[224] Other skeletons turned up in later decades on the Mouse River but too far from the event to determine if they were victims of the Montana Stranglers.[225]

Camping at Dogden Butte

On Saturday, November 15, three ranchers from Mouse River camped at Dogden Butte on their return trip from Bismarck for supplies. These ranchers also worked as teamsters, hauling goods to the new settlements on the Mouse. Because the cowboys were watching all who passed through the area, they rode up to check this outfit out as well. Recognizing them as friendly, and because it was the end of the day, the vigilantes joined the local ranchers' camp. Tom Berry, Johnny Pendroy and Marion Pace had seen the posse at the Berry ranch a week before with Ravenwood, Bates and Gardipee, their former mail carrier.[226]

They likely spent the night on the strip of land between Camp and Strawberry Lake, a typical stopping point on the Totten Trail. Berry said the three horse thieves wore crude white hats made of flannel fashioned by the vigilantes.[227] This would distinguish them from the rest of the group. Perhaps this was a safety precaution. They would not want to shoot the wrong guy if someone tried to escape.

Their cook pulled out a coffee pot and a skillet from a packhorse. He whipped up hot coffee, pancakes and bacon. This served as supper for the group. Afterward, Gardipee, speaking to whoever would listen, said, "I will go as far as Washburn and return from that point." He was kind of telling and kind of hoping. People in Washburn knew him. Perhaps Sheriff Satterlund would put a stop to this. In reply, one cowboy carelessly remarked, "When Gardipee got as far as Washburn he would conclude to go on."[228]

The cowboys had no tents; they slept on the ground with their saddle as their pillow and wrapped themselves with one wool bed roll on what had to be cold November nights. The captives were in chains and roped together with lariats. They slept tied on the frozen ground.[229] What a miserable time these three must have experienced—locked in irons for eight days with no comforts or protection from the November wind.

The following morning, breakfast was the same as supper—coffee, pancakes and bacon. After the meal, the cowboys packed up to move on. Gardipee spoke to Tom Berry as they were readied to leave: "Tell my wife goodbye, I do not think I will be back for a long time."

It is said that at this comment, Flopping Bill looked back and laughed.[230]

HANGMAN'S POINT

After the cowboys broke camp at Dogden Butte on Sunday morning, November 16, they headed south. Gardipee, Ravenwood and Bates had begun their final ride. This entourage must have created quite a sight. The prisoners were pushed out front, three ashen riders in shackles, wearing odd-looking white hats. Big Flopping Bill, sitting tall in his saddle, followed close behind with his Winchester draped across his waist. He was riding point on the herd.[231] He kept a watchful eye on his prize. A herd of 117 horses with Montana brands all trailed out, loping over the rolling prairie hills and around the many frozen sloughs. The herd was flanked on the sides and behind by fifteen stern-faced cowboys.

The crew rolled past the picturesque shorelines of Strawberry, Long and Crooked Lakes. Ten miles they rode that morning. About halfway down the three-mile-long final lake in the chain, they came to a place where a thin point of land jutted over halfway across the narrow body of water. After they started out, Gardipee may have found some reason to hope when he realized the direction they were headed. Washburn was at the end of this trail. The people there knew him. Sheriff Satterlund would make certain he got a fair trial. If only he could make it to Washburn, he would go no farther.

FAST-FORWARD TO MAY 1886

In the spring of 1886, two men from the Washburn area went to Crooked Lake to fish for perch. They found a promising spot off a long narrow point that put them out in the middle of the lake. With gunny sacks strung over their shoulders and long poles, they waded waist-deep. They were hauling in the yellow perch slabs and had caught about twenty-five pounds when one of them snagged something. As he pulled his line, human remains floated to the surface.[232]

The two men went straight to Sheriff Satterlund in Washburn. On his arrival at Crooked Lake, Satterlund discovered three beaten bodies, hands and feet still tied, and a bullet hole through each head. They had been executed. Although the corpses were decayed, the sheriff identified the remains as the three horse thieves taken from Mouse River country. Bates was recognized for his size 12 boots. Their bodies had been pushed down under the November ice forming on this prairie lake and then tied to the pencil reeds and cattails. Satterlund collected the deceased and took them to Washburn.[233]

Hangman's Point has been the name of this location from that time on. We return to November 1884 and McLean County.

The Stranglers were later spotted in Coal Harbor, McLean County. It was noted that Gardipee, Bates and Ravenwood were no longer with them.[234] Stanley Ravenwood was no. 51, John Bates no. 52 and Francis Gardipee no. 53 murdered since October 1883. But the Montana Stranglers were not finished in Dakota Territory just yet.

Clubfoot Jack Wilson

After the cowboys finished their deadly work at Crooked Lake, they moved across McLean County to the Missouri. Somewhere near Victoria they collected Jack Wilson, aka Clubfoot Wilson.[235] Wilson had been a wood hawk and a horse trader, but he developed the bad habit of first stealing horses before trading them.[236]

In October 1884, Wilson was caught selling stolen horses in Montana. He went before a judge in Glendive, was convicted, escaped jail and headed back to his home in Dakota Territory, where the vigilantes found him in late November.[237] The *Bismarck Tribune* says the vigilantes attempted to retrieve a reward from the people at Stanton, DT, but they refused to pay.[238] The paper also says Wilson then disappeared and leaves the impression that he was no. 54 on our death toll, but this is not the case.

Why is hard to understand, but the Stranglers must have let him go. Their decisions are hard to decipher sometimes. You get the impression that Clubfoot was a pathetic petty thief that people did not take seriously enough to hang.

We know they did not kill him because, in 1885, Clubfoot again stole two black mares in the Stanton area and then headed to the Little Missouri for his escape into the Bad Lands. When he realized he was being overtaken, he shot the two mares. He was soon captured by Sheriff McGahan of Stanton and put in shackles. The rules of the day would suggest he had earned a hanging. Instead, the sheriff hauled him back to Stanton.

Lucky for Clubfoot, he was one of only a handful of citizens in Mercer County who could vote. On that day, a hotly contested decision was being made to determine whether the town of Stanton or Causey would become the county seat. Legend has it that the vote was an even split until the sheriff brought Clubfoot to town in chains. A tie breaker was needed. Clubfoot may have been pathetic, but he was not a complete fool. He wisely voted for

Stanton, which is the county seat to this day. He was then told to vamoose as his reward for good behavior.[239]

The Kid and Two Stringed Hanna

Somewhere northwest of Bismarck, Flopping Bill stumbled onto two men who had escaped from the jail in his hometown of Maiden, Montana, on October 11. Someone let them go. Who or how was a mystery. The escapees attempted to put as much distance as possible between themselves and Montana. They probably would have gotten away with it but for the dumb luck that this stock detective from their county chanced upon them hiding out in Dakota. One of them was a young man named George Outhwaite, alias the Kid. He came from a very fine family in Nebraska. His father was a business owner, well known and respected. The Kid chose the life of a horse thief and ended up in the Meagher County, Montana jail. If this jailbreaking convicted horse thief had been a Métis, they would have hanged him with little debate. But since he was from a respected family, he got different treatment. Bill would haul him eight hundred miles, over a month and a half in tow, all the way back to the Meagher County jail.

Bill did another curious thing. The Kid had broken out of jail with a man named Two Stringed Joe Hanna, who was convicted of murder. Joe shot and killed George Nelson in Barker, Montana. Joe Hanna had wealthy relatives, and it was obvious someone paid someone to leave locks open.[240]

There was a reward of $500 offered for Hanna's capture. Flopping Bill just let him go. On Bill's return home, he explained his reason was that he did not believe that a stock detective was authorized to arrest a murderer. Joe Hanna sent a message back with Bill to the authorities in Meagher County that he would turn himself in if he could be given a different judge. I suspect Bill did not think Hanna was guilty of murder. When you read the newspaper accounts of Hanna's story, it does sound more like self-defense against an insane man. With some kinds of people, Bill could be merciful.

La Page Becomes Scarce

Now, in contrast, the vigilantes continued up the Missouri River toward Berthold, the trading post for the Three Affiliated Tribes. The people from Berthold reported the cowboys had the Kid, and somewhere along the

Missouri River, they collected another man named La Page. There was a place between Fort Stevenson and Berthold called "No-man's-land." It was an un-surveyed section of the county and rumored to conceal one of those camps used by outlaws. Perhaps they found La Page there.

In 1886, the *Fort Benton River Press* mentions an Edward La Page being sought for stealing horses. He had a brother who was a notorious horse thief who "made himself scarce a few years ago."[241] According to the people at Berthold, the Stranglers took La Page up into the hills for two days and then came back without him. He has been scarce ever since.[242] La Page is no. 54 and the final killing in Dakota Territory by the Montana Stranglers. La Page was another Métis.

Hunting Parties Report

Most of the information after Hangman's Point comes from a party of sport hunters out of Bismarck who were returning home, coming down the Missouri after a five-week outing. They stayed one week at Grinnell Landing. (Can't help but wonder what they were hunting at Grinnell's bar for a week.) Grinnell told them he was expecting the vigilantes and seemed confident about what I believe would have been a second visit. The vigilantes held up the Bismarck hunters just west of Berthold near the Slides. A ferry operator named Farr was with the hunters, and he too was detained but longer because he had allowed horse thieves to use his ferry at Knife River. The encounter of this group of Bismarck sportsmen with the Montana Stranglers would have been about November 27. They gave their report to the *Bismarck Weekly Tribune* on their return on Tuesday, December 9.[243]

The Baldwin and Mathews Ranches

On about November 28, the Stranglers arrived at the ranch of Charles Baldwin at Nesson Flats about twenty-one miles east of present Williston. They spent the night. Baldwin reported they were driving a herd of about one hundred horses, all with Montana brands. But he said there were forty vigilantes in the group. Baldwin told this story and recorded it many decades later, so his numbers may have grown over the years.

Grinnell's place was down the river a few miles to the east from Baldwin. There is no record of a second visit. Nothing happened. Grinnell mentioned to the Bismarck sportsmen that he had twenty people working for him. Perhaps he had them all well armed and ready. One newspaper article said he had the place booby trapped with explosives should the Stranglers snoop through his corrals. One thing seems clear about Flopping Bill. He did not care to enter a fair fight. Whenever he makes a move, the numbers are always stacked in his favor. Bill knew what it felt like to be shot. It happened once; he would not have it happen again.

Next, they went to Bob Mathews's ranch along the Missouri at the Little Muddy, which is the location of present-day Williston. They spent a night camping at his ranch.[244]

Fort Buford and Home

The last stop in Dakota Territory was at Fort Buford about the first week of December. Billy Adams recalled seeing Flopping Bill's posse at the local eatery. He counted seventeen in the committee. In addition, they had with them George Outhwaite (the Kid). George had been an acquaintance of Adams's from Decatur, Nebraska, and he recognized him.[245]

From here, Flopping Bill's posse reentered Montana Territory. The normal trail would have been to follow the Yellowstone River through Glendive. Bill arrived in Miles City on January 5. We can assume it took December and January to return the horses to their proper owners through the proper channels. The last report from this expedition came out in the *Mineral Argus* of Maiden, Montana, January 22, 1885.

Summing Up Bill Cantrell's Work in Dakota Territory October to December 1884

He traveled well over one thousand miles by train, horseback and possibly a riverboat. He had six confirmed kills, left one suspicious skeleton, one rumored kill and one missing person who was last seen in his custody. Bill terrorized eight cowboys on various nester ranches. He gave George Grinnell a scare, turned one convicted murderer and one convicted horse thief free. He brought home one white privileged horse thief. His posse returned 117 stolen Montana horses to their rightful owners.

For many years, this folk song was commonly heard in the Minot area:

The Capture of Horse Thieves
By John Barton,
As printed in the Burlington Republican, *November 20, 1884.*

It was on the fourth of November, in the year of '84
We were overtaken by eighteen cowboys,
I'm sure there were no more,
Overtaken by eighteen cowboys, indeed it was too late,
The thieves that they were after were Ravenwood and Baites.

Chorus
Young men acruising
I'll have you to beware,
To leave off horse stealing,
And live upon the square.
The marshal he is ready.
And the cowboys they are nigh,
They'll run you off from Burlington,
To hang you up to dry.

It was on the morning of the fifth, just at the break of day,
Ravenwood went to the barn and saddled up the gray,
He rode down to the camp where the boys did stay,
And there he talked in French until he gave himself away.

On the sixth of November at the Dogdens they did stay,
Ravenwood wrote McDonald, and thus to him did say,
Take care of all my letters for I'm agoing away,
I fear I shall not read them until the Judgement Day.

9
UNHAPPY ENDINGS

Now you Cain are cursed from the ground, which has opened its mouth to receive your brother's blood from your hand. When you cultivate the ground, it will no longer yield its strength to you; you will be a vagrant and a wanderer on the earth.
—*Genesis 4*

This is a true story, and true stories don't always have happy endings. This one does not. That damn prairie wind is brutal.

The Hacketts

Let's return to Edmund Hackett and his youthful bride, Leah. What could go wrong here? He was wed to a beautiful woman whom he seemed truly to love. She had security, money, two homes—one on a river and one with lakefront views—and a hopeful future. By all appearances, she held a true, deep, abiding love for Edmund. Together, they shared a son.

Edmund's many ambitious endeavors made him a busy man, so he was gone from his wife more than he was home. She was only twenty-one years old and caring for a six-month-old baby boy. She probably faced some guilt and some personal and public shame over her out-of-wedlock pregnancy. There also might have been trouble between her and Hackett's son, Ed Jr. Gossip of the day suggested she was being worked very hard, not only taking care of her baby but also cooking and cleaning for Hackett and the six men he had in his employ at Souris City. Gossipers called it slave labor. These pressures took a toll on her mental health.[246]

The family was facing other pressures. Edmund's popularity was waning in the Villard area. Back in October 1884, when they created McHenry County, he and Colonel Towner used some political shenanigans to appoint themselves the first commissioners.[247] They were scheming to establish the county seat at Souris City. This move would cement their power and control in the region, but it did not set well with the rest of the local population. Eugene Fish became a vocal enemy of Hackett.[248] We may connect this to the way Hackett had treated the Gardipees. The Fish family and the Gardipees were not only close neighbors but also friends. Fish shared with the Gardipees the same dispute over land with Hackett.

Christmas 1884 would be the darkest of Edmund Hackett's life. His wedding anniversary was December 10. Edmund was in Bismarck and not with Leah on their first anniversary. Leah was not well. She was living in this isolated area, Souris City, with her husband mostly absent. She was clearly suffering from postpartum depression. That is a dangerous cocktail.

As the Montana Stranglers were heading back into Montana, a darkness was falling on the Hackett family. On an early December evening, Leah came to the Fish ranch, distraught and saying Edmund was going to kill her and the baby was endangered. Fish galloped to the Hackett house, which was less than a mile away. The baby was there, safe but alone. Fish returned with the child and that night took Leah by wagon to friends near Minnewaukan sixty miles east.[249]

He left Leah and her child with the McDonalds six miles from Minnewaukan. During the day on Thursday, December 11, a stranger dropped by, which spooked Leah. She fled to the nearby Gibson home. At 3:00 a.m. on Friday, Leah left her baby with the Gibsons and ran to Minnewaukan, to the hotel called the Trafton House.

Here she poured out her domestic troubles, claiming Ed Hackett Jr. threatened to kill her. The Traftons thought her rational and believed her. She offered to work off her board until her husband could come to square the bill. They all knew Hackett would be good for it. Traftons sent a liveryman to fetch her baby from the Gibson house some five miles away.

Leah went to work in the kitchen cutting bread.

"You sure got a dull lot of knives," she said.

"The bread knife is probably the sharpest," Mrs. Trafton replied.

At this, Leah whetted the bread knife against another, turned to the mirror, placed the knife on her throat and cut through her windpipe. Mrs. Trafton looked away from her cooking just in time to see and grabbed Leah's hand before she could reach an artery. This saved her life. Mrs. Trafton screamed for help, and they carried Leah to a couch.

She whispered, "I would like to see my husband. Don't tell my mother."

Mrs. Trafton asked, "Where is your husband?"

"At Mouse River. He can get here with a fast horse."

"Leah, why did you do this?"

"I had such great trouble it drove me mad."[250]

Hidden in her pocket, they found this note:

> *EDMUND:*
> *I do not know the secret.*
> *I am innocent. That child is yours—I swear it. I die easy.*
> *Edmund, see what your eldest son has done for both of us.*
> *I want Mrs. Welch to take the baby and raise it.*
> *Your son Edward is a scamp.*
> *This is death to part with you.*[251]

When word first got out about Leah, the rumor was spread by the newspaper that Hackett and his son murdered her. Fish and others were out looking for Hackett, and if they had found him, they planned to lynch him.

In fairness, it does not appear that Leah's accusations against Edmund Hackett were entirely true. Leah's tragic action hit him hard. She improved for a time. He was struggling with whether to send her to the mental institution in Jamestown, to her parents, or to build a special home there in Minnewaukan and care for her himself.[252] None of this would be necessary. She lingered for a month from her wound. In mid-January, the Devils Lake paper printed this:

> *Edmund Hackett…arrived in the city…and stated that Mrs. Hackett died on the Thursday previous. Death was the result of inflammation of the lungs caused by inhaling cold air through the self-inflicted wound in the throat, the wound refusing to heal.*[253]

That damned wind blew hard over Dakota in 1884, leaving a bleak and bitter place. They fell under the curse. It was winter, but there would be no

Christmas in this home this year.[254] Edmund Hackett gave his baby boy to JK and Mary Salisbury, a childless family in Minnewaukan. They did not keep him. His final disposition is not known.[255]

Land Disputes

It was a sad time too for Caroline Gardipee—her husband gone and with no idea where he might be, she faced an uncertain future with a powerful neighbor who wanted to dispossess her of her land. She may have feared that no one cared about her well-being or what was just for her.

With Francis Gardipee now disposed of, Hackett set out that winter, even as his wife was dying, to secure as his own the land on which the Gardipees had been squatting for many years. As squatters, they would have no deed to prove ownership. Hackett filed a preemption claim on this property. Having made improvements, he offered to purchase the land from the government. He sought in this fashion to steal official ownership. Hackett and Colonel Towner were speculating where the railroad would cross the Mouse River. They were locking up land at Villard, Souris City, and farther upstream Towner had made acquisitions.

Caroline Gardipee knew they had taken her husband away but heard only rumors of what had happened to him. She now must face this other problem alone, adding to her grief and uncertainty about how she would care for her children. The most powerful man in her community was trying to take her land. She did not read or write[256] and was facing new laws and a foreign culture. She may not even have been able to speak English well. I would imagine Hackett thought she would be an easy pick.

Hackett found himself in court in Devils Lake over this in March 1885. Caroline Gardipee gained the legal help of the postmaster of Newport, C.E. Jones. He defended her case against Hackett and won.[257] Not everyone was prejudiced against the Métis. Some people could be just and honorable.

Hackett was also in court the same week in a land dispute with Eugene Fish. Fish must really have hated Hackett. He brought a concealed gun to the courtroom, and during the proceedings, attempted to shoot Hackett. They tackled Fish before he got a shot off, arrested him, and he was thrown in jail.[258]

Hackett did not stay much longer in the area. He sold his land to James Eaton, dusted the snow from his boots like thousands of others have done in Dakota and headed south to warmer, less windy climates.

Métis family with Red River Carts in Western Dakota Territory 1883. *Collection: A Folder: 0000.000 Item: 4365 00001 SHSND.*

They never built the Bismarck, Mouse River, Turtle Mountain and Manitoba Railroad. The cities of Villard and Hackett Falls (Souris City) have not shown up on a map for over one hundred years. Nothing came of Hackett's dream.

Hackett left Dakota Territory in 1885. In his new home in Alabama, he came up with two useful inventions. In 1889, he filed a patent for an automatic railroad car coupler. He also invented and patented a potato digger and sacker all in one. He moved to Guthrie, Oklahoma, to manufacture the devices. Newspapers of the time effused how rich Hackett would become. But Hard-Luck Hackett got nothing from any of it. The economy had another terrible downturn in the 1890s, and no one had any money to purchase his products. He and Ed Jr. wandered to Canada and worked as carpenters in Saskatchewan for a time.[259]

He made one last desperate attempt to gain his fortune. He and his son moved to Kalispell, Montana, to search for gold. Here, his son preceded him in death. A sad note can be found in the Kalispell paper. The county approved Edmund Hackett to receive a six-dollar-per-month veteran's pension.[260] At age seventy-two, that is all he had left. He died practically penniless on October 7, 1905, found alone along the road lying under his horse and wagon.[261] The death certificate stated cause of death to be a fatty heart.[262]

THE GARDIPEES

"King John." Sheriff John Satterlund of Washburn, Dakota Territory. *McLean County Museum, Washburn, North Dakota.*

What became of Caroline and her children? In the Scrip records from Duhamel, Alberta, a John Gariepy lists his father, Fransais; mother, Caroline; and siblings, Josue, Adele and Antoinette, all as deceased in the 1890s. It appears Caroline remarried about 1885.[263] Perhaps Caroline moved west to join the other Métis communities during the Riel Rebellion. Eventually, Caroline must have learned what happened to her husband. I hope her neighbors passed on to her that her husband's last thoughts were about her.

As we have said, fishermen in May 1886 snagged a body in Crooked Lake. The manner in which Gardipee was kidnapped and then murdered is bad enough. What the people of Washburn did with his corpse furthers the indignity. Gardipee's words were oddly prophetic—he said he would go to Washburn and go no farther. Records show that Sheriff Satterlund collected the decayed remains, brought them back to town and then threw them out the back door of the jailhouse and left them on the ground.[264] One can imagine how wild animals, dogs and souvenir hunters carried off their bones until they were no more.

God created all human beings in His own image, and all deserve certain rights and respect as human beings regardless of race, creed or even their crimes. These men were not without guilt, but they did not deserve to be killed and then treated with such indignity.

This was unjust.

From March to May 1885, the Métis and other members of the Iron Alliance made their own last stand at Batoche, Saskatchewan. Led by their spiritual leader Louis Riel, they attempted to establish a place for their nation. Many of the Gardipee family fought alongside Riel.[265] They battled valiantly but to no good end. The government of Canada hanged Riel. Their revolution was quickly over. The Métis as a people disappeared on both sides of the Medicine Line until the 1960s. Neither the Canadian nor the United States governments recognized them as Indian, and communities did not treat them as white. An entire people lost their identity. It is not until the last few decades that they had reestablished who they are.[266]

FLOPPING BILL

William Cantrell worked until 1890 as a stock detective in Montana and seems to have done so with a positive reputation.[267] The hanging of horse thieves continued, but not by the stock detectives. As Montana became more settled, under the rule of law, such activities would likely have led to his own hanging, and Bill Cantrell was no fool. He adjusted to the changing times. Did killing twenty people satisfy his bitterness and need for revenge? Probably not, but he did not kill again. People can change.

In 1888, Bill met and married Mary Battle, the daughter of a sheep rancher near Alder, Montana. They had three children, and he proved to

Montana Stock Inspectors, 1885. *Back row, left to right*: James L. Cox, Charles D. Hard and William "Floppin' Bill" Cantrell; *front row*: Harry Lander, Charles W. Barney, Wilson D. "Billy" Smith and Tom A. Matthews. *Abbott Family photograph collection, Montana Historical Society*.

Mouse River Cowboys. 1880s. *Collection:10147 Folder: 0007.000 Item: 0008 SHSND.*

be a good father. His son Leyland showed musical talent, so Bill traveled to Boston and purchased the boy a piano. He had it shipped around Cape Horn, through San Francisco, to Salt Lake City and then to Montana at great expense. The young man became an accomplished pianist.[268]

In 1900, Bill was moving his family to Kansas City, closer to his childhood home, and it was here that he had a bit of hard luck himself on September 25 at age fifty-two. He was on a train in Kansas City, Missouri, hauling cattle. Bill jumped off to water his stock, and his boot got jammed in the track. The train struck and killed him. Most of his body remained affixed to the train as it picked up speed, heading down the track. No one noticed until the train reached Miami, Oklahoma, about 160 miles away. They buried what they had of his remains in Miami.[269]

One cannot help but think about the Buddhist concept of karma when you reflect on the lives of Bill Cantrell and Edmund Hackett. I don't believe in it, but it gives you pause to consider that perhaps someone is keeping score.

EPILOGUE

So now we know how Hangman's Point got its name. And in knowing, perhaps we bring just a bit of justice for those who were killed here. They were not innocent of all crimes, but certainly they had done nothing that justified their murder.

Although the hill is still present, Dogden Butte has all but disappeared. Absolutely no one would even think to call them the Dogden Mountains. In the 1800s, Dogden Butte was a prominent and noticeable place. An important landmark on the Road to the Mandan, followed by many early explorers, all of whom mention it. Here the Dakota watched for their enemies and pounced down on them. For this reason, it was a place noted and feared by those who traveled nearby. It was a place where the Métis always found buffalo, a landmark on the Totten Trail between Forts Stevenson and Totten on the wagon trail to Montana. Everyone who passed by would see ahead and realize where they were.

Most people who live in central North Dakota today do not even know where or what it is. It has lost its sense of place. For persons who have seen the Rocky Mountains or the Grand Canyon, a prairie hill is now insignificant by comparison. So, it has disappeared unless someone points it out and tells its stories. The Grand Coteau is no longer considered grand. It is just a low range of hills on the horizon as you travel west across North Dakota.

For centuries, Dogden Butte was a place of warfare and death. It was holy ground to the Mandan peoples, but it was also a battleground. Down through the years, people lost their lives through violence at this place. About a year

The prairie between Dogden Butte and Strawberry Lake, North Dakota. There is nothing there, and that is the point. *Photo by Eric Berget.*

after Gardipee's death, one more man was murdered at Dog Den Butte, but that is for another book. He was the last.

As the new European immigrants homesteaded the land, the killing ended. The Norwegian Lutherans, German Russian Baptists, German Catholics who filled in this once empty wilderness paid attention to the rule of law and the command "thou shall not kill," so for generations the homicide rate in North Dakota was one of the lowest in the nation and even the world. (Gun ownership is one of the highest in the nation. Go figure?) The law and the belief in life's value were engraved on their consciences for generations, and in a place where murder and violence had reigned for centuries, now such things became rare events.[270]

The residents of today forgot the stories of the past. Dogden Butte faded into the landscape as the plow turned over the prairie and they tamed the wild places. These homesteading peasants were fruitful, and they multiplied. One set of the author's grandparents at their death had 230 living descendants. They sent out from this bountiful land a crop of people that have had a far greater effect both in numbers and in influence than what you might expect from such a windy, inauspicious homeland.

Peoples continue to come and go. The homesteading Europeans are now being replaced by other ethnicities from around the world, and the story continues.

NOTES

Introduction

1. This is a book of factual history, but periodically, I speculate just a little on what might have been based on what we know. These two really did find the bodies while fishing; the details were added for color. This is done sparingly in the book.
2. "A Daring Capture," *Jamestown Weekly Alert*, April 23, 1885.
3. It is possible one of the lawmen on his trail was Liver Eating Johnson. He was sheriff in Coulson, Montana, about the time this murder occurred.
4. Two examples are *Missouri River Breaks* and *The Ballad of Lefty Brown*.
5. *Post* (Billings, MT), August 16, 1883, 5.

Chapter 1

6. Brown, *McHenry County*, 37.
7. Mrs. Tom (Belle) Berry, January 9,1 937, MSS10147, Box 006, John C. Eaton Papers, 1908 to 1958, SHSND [hereafter Berry, SHSND].
8. Brown, *McHenry County*, 37.
9. De Trobriand, *Military Life in Dakota*, 192, 193, 224.
10. Smith, *Champion Buffalo Hunter*, "Part II Introduction to the Frontier. Carrying the Mail," Kindle.

11. ND State Highway 41 from Velva to Turtle Lake would roughly approximate "The Road to the Mandan." Exactly where this trail went is not clear. There were likely several versions. The description given is an educated guess.
12. Barkwell, "Dakota-Métis Battle."
13. Kelly and Quaife, *Yellowstone Kelly*, chapter 2.
14. There are many Métis named Francis Gardipee. I believe this to be the Francis Gardipee born in 1842 to Louis and Angelic Gardupe listed in the 1860 census. I cannot be certain. This man's wife was Caroline, and they had three children. The name is spelled in countless ways: Gurapiey, Gardipea, Gardipe and Gardupe, to name just a few.
15. In 1864, General Sully passed through hundreds of thousands of bison as he traveled south of Dogden Butte following the Road to the Mandan, headed to Fort Rice. This massive migratory Red River bison herd disappeared in the winter of 1866–67. So sudden a population collapse could not have been from over hunting.
16. Kelly and Quaife, *Yellowstone Kelly*, chapter 2.
17. The receding ice of the Laurentide Glacier created a complex of glacial wetlands that wildlife biologists today call the prairie pothole region. It is the North American duck factory, producing the millions of ducks, geese, swans and other shorebirds that fly north and south each year. The area around Dogden Butte is some of the finest duck-producing land on planet Earth.
18. The coldest temperature ever recorded in North Dakota, -60°F, on February 15, 1936, was in Parshall, just seventy miles from Dogden Butte.
19. In my childhood, the North Dakota wind was frequently referenced with two syllables.
20. *Bismarck Tribune*, April 7, 1882.
21. Section 31 of Newport Township, McHenry County.
22. Article written by son of John Pendroy, MSS10147, Box 006, John C. Eaton Papers, 1908 to 1958, SHSND.
23. A colony of African Americans also settled in the village of Pendroy in 1884. Most stayed only one winter. One man from the colony, J.H. Vaughn, remained and opened a general store. Wick, *North Dakota Place Names*, 152. Other herds of cattle and horses arrived in 1883. On page 26 is the image of the Thursby ranch herd newly arrived at the Mouse River.
24. The *Devils Lake Inter-Ocean*, November 22, 1884, gave this name as Frank Burno, certainly misspelled. Bruneau is a Métis name. Also, could be Bonneau. See *Métis Dictionary of Biography*, vol. B, compiled by Lawrence J. Barkwell, 92.

25. Daschuk, *Clearing the Plains*, chapter 7.
26. Smith, *Champion Buffalo Hunter*, loc. 1902, Kindle. Smith recounts the cold-blooded murder of Dutch Pete by Aleck Brown at Spaniard Point Woodyard on the Missouri in 1873.
27. Ludwig Watne of Washburn observed Gardipee in the fall of 1883 putting out these stakes in preparation for delivering the mail that winter. State Agency Record Historical Data Project Pioneer Biography #30529, SHSND.
28. Snow blindness, also called arc eye or photokeratitis, is a painful eye condition caused by overexposure to ultraviolet (UV) light. When too much UV light hits the transparent cornea, it essentially gives your cornea a sunburn. Snow blindness symptoms can be disorienting. This was a constant danger to winter travelers in the Northwest.
29. Brown, *McHenry County*, 37.
30. The term *missing middle* was coined by the missiologist Paul Hiebert.
31. The heavenlies are referenced at Ephesians 1:20, 2:6, 3:10, 6:12.

Chapter 2

32. "Hackett and McLean Were First Mayors," *Bismarck Tribune*, April 7, 1934; Eriksmoen, "Friends Help Hackett."
33. *Bismarck Tribune*, February 28, 1877.
34. Eriksmoen, "Friends Help Hackett."
35. Elderedge, *Third New Hampshire*, 816.
36. *Bismarck Tribune*, April 7, 1934.
37. *Kalispell Bee*, October 10, 1905.
38. Robinson, *History of North Dakota*. "The Too-Much mistake is my name for too many farms, too many miles of railroads and roads, too many towns, banks, schools, colleges, churches, and governmental institutions… beyond the ability of the state to maintain."
39. *Bismarck Tribune*, September 14, 1922. First picture of Bismarck includes Hackett with long hair.
40. Lounsberry, "Of the Burned Block at Bismarck," 50, 51.
41. Custer, *Following the Guidon*, 319.
42. *Bismarck Weekly Tribune*, November 5, 1880.
43. *Bismarck Weekly Tribune*, April 19, 1879.
44. *Bismarck Tribune*, December 9, 1881.
45. *Bismarck Tribune*, April 21, 1882

46. We are meant to read gold here. Métis told of finding some small nuggets. This entire area along the Mouse River in McHenry County has gold. The Denbigh Deposit contains a very fine gold sand, but no one has found a deposit rich enough to be profitable. See Bluemle, "Gold in North Dakota."
47. *Bismarck Tribune*, April 7, 1882.
48. Ibid.
49. *Bismarck Tribune*, April 20, 1883.
50. *Bismarck Tribune*, April 7, 1882.
51. Gourneau, *History of the Turtle Mountain Band*, 9.
52. *Bismarck Tribune*, April 7, 1882.

Chapter 3

53. *Yellowstone Kelly*, Gordon, Douglas, director, Warner Brothers, 1959; *The Legend of Kootenai Brown* (renamed *Showdown at Williams Creek*) Kroeker, Alan, director, Crescent Entertainment, 1991.
54. William Cantrell, born August 3, 1848, McMinn, Tennessee, to Mary Jane and Joseph Cantrell, U.S. Census, 1850.
55. *Arkansas Democrat*, December 17, 1898. p.7
56. Barrows, *U-Bet*, 213. Ironside is probably a reference to Oliver Cromwell, a strong religious leader who was also murderous. Bill was also a strong leader without the religion.
57. Joseph Taylor and Vic Smith say they heard this directly from Bill. We know that Bill's dad was not Quantrill's brother. Did Bill just make this up? That is possible.
58. Smith, *Champion Buffalo Hunter*, loc. 2092–92, Kindle.
59. Taylor, *Kaleidoscopic Lives*, 87.
60. Gordon, "Steamboats, Woodhawks and War," 37.
61. Ibid., 35.
62. Taylor, *Sketches of Frontier and Indian Life*, loc. 1058, Kindle.
63. Taylor, *Kaleidoscopic Lives*, 87.
64. Gordon, "Steamboats, Woodhawks and War," 32, 33.
65. Chardon, *Chardon's Journal at Fort Clark*, 123, and following have a description of the horrible pandemic of 1837, which decimated the Plains tribes.
66. Taylor, *Sketches of Frontier and Indian Life*, loc. 1058, Kindle.
67. Wilmot P. Sanford Diary, 335–78.

68. Ibid.; Taylor, *Kaleidoscopic Lives*, 87.
69. This necklace held a decorative skull supposedly given to Grinnell by Cole Younger.
70. Innis, "Act of God."
71. Barkwell, "Nehiyaw Pwat (Iron Alliance)."
72. Abbott, Smith and Tyler, *We Pointed Them North*, 123–24.
73. Taylor, *Kaleidoscopic Lives*, 89–90. I am skeptical about Taylor's account. He might be borrowing from the *National Police Gazette* account from August 1884. It claimed a Nosey Bartel was the last man hanged at the Musselshell camps. The *NPG* account appears to be almost an entire fabrication; Taylor's account of what he did not personally see might be a fabrication also.
74. McCord, *Calling the Brands*, 43.
75. *Mineral Argus*, January 1885.

Chapter 4

76. Pfeifer, "Roots of Rough Justice."
77. *Big Stone City Herald*, July 4, 1884.
78. *Harrisburg Telegraph*, January 21, 1889.
79. Charles T. Staley (1863–1942), Manuscript, 1934, 1458. 20111 OCLC 17998480, SHSND [hereafter Staley, SHSND].
80. *Bismarck Tribune*, May 16, 1884.
81. Ibid.
82. *Jamestown Weekly Alert*, August 29, 1884.
83. *Bismarck Weekly Tribune*, May 16, 1884.
84. Dr. John W. Robinson (b. 1879), Tape #4 573A & B, at 1:25:10, SHSND [hereafter Robinson, SHSND].
85. Staley, SHSND.
86. Tom O'Neil was not alone. He had picked up another young man who had jumped off a boat and thrown in with Tom. Fortunately, the vigilantes realized this man's innocence and let him go.
87. Robinson, SHSND.
88. *Washburn Times*, June 27, 1884.
89. Taylor, *Kaleidoscopic Lives*, 94.
90. *Bismarck Weekly Tribune*, June 27, 1884.
91. Artz, "Eris of the West."
92. *Washburn Times*, July 11, 1884.

Chapter 5

93. There are several things that support this idea. Yam James from the Musselshell gangs was reported to be with Jim Smith from White Earth Dakota Territory when they raided the Whipple's payroll wagon. Dutch Charley came from the Musselshell gangs to set up in Mouse River. It appears the Métis gangs were heading to Dutch Charley's relay on occasions when caught. Red Mike with Buffalo ran east from the Musselshell area into Dakota to Grinnell Landing and Jim Smith's hideout.
94. Taylor, *Kaleidoscopic Lives*, 89.
95 *Washburn Times*, December 14, 1883.
96. *Burlington Centennial*, 23.
97. See page 124 in chapter 8.
98. *Burlington Centennial*, 23.
99. *Jamestown Weekly Alert*, April 23, 1885. There seems to be some question as to whether the person captured was in fact Dutch Charley. See also the *Daily Yellowstone Journal* (Miles City, MT), April 27, May 9 and May 28, 1885; Burdick, *Jim Johnson Pioneer*, 30.
100. Williams, *Pioneer Days of Washburn*, 53, 54.
101. See page 133 in chapter 8
102. *History of Mercer County*, 25.
103. Ibid., 27.
104. Burdick, *Jim Johnson Pioneer*, 28.
105. *Bismarck Tribune*, October 5, 1883.
106. Breeling, *When the Trail Was New*, 51.
107. Ibid., 52.
108. Ibid.
109. Fort Buford Post Report Record of Events, December 4, 1883, SHSND.
110. Smith, *Champion Buffalo Hunter*, loc. 2105–6, Kindle.
111. Fort Buford Post Report Record of Events, SHSND.
112. *Devil's Lake Inter-Ocean*, November 22, 1884.
113. *Washburn Times*, December 15, 1883.
114. Ibid.
115. Tye, "Some Things About the Vigilante Raid."
116. *Sun River Sun*, August 21, 1884.
117. See page 61. Jim Smith hits McLean County in the spring of 1884.
118. *Bismarck Weekly Tribune*, June 27, 1884.
119. *Washburn Times*, June 27, 1884.
120. See chapter 4, page 66. *Washburn Times*, July 11, 1884.

121. *Emmons County Record*, July 25, 1884; *Wahpeton Times*, June 13, 1884.
122. *Bad Lands Cowboy*, March 6, 1884.
123. Sewall, *Bill Sewall's Story of TR*, 31ff.
124. *Jamestown Weekly Alert*, August 22, 1884, quoting the *Washburn Times*; Williams, *Pioneer Days of Washburn, North Dakota and Vicinity*, 54.
125. *Devil's Lake Inter-Ocean*, November 22, 1884. Also referenced by Williams, *Pioneer Days of Washburn*, 54.
126. Staley, SHSND.

Chapter 6

127. To give some perspective, in the year 2020 there were over 700 homicides in Chicago, Illinois. The Old West could be brutal, but it does not hold a candle to our cities today. On the other hand, based on percent of population, the rate of killings on the upper Missouri country in 1884 was much higher than Chicago.
128. Milner and O'Connor, *As Big as the West*, 307ff.
129. Daschuk, *Clearing the Plains*, chapter 7.
130. Fred Ojers, *Great Falls Tribune*, September 26, 1926, as quoted in Mueller, "Central Montana Vigilante Raids."
131. One of these, Private James Birch, died three months later at Fort Buford, very likely from this wound.
132. Norman, *Uncommon Journey*, 168.
133. *Daily Enterprise*, June 3, 1884; Was this the Jim Smith referenced in chapter 6 and elsewhere, the leader of the infamous Jim Smith gang? I believe it was; there are no more references to him in newspapers after the summer of 1884.
134. Morris, *Rise of Theodore Roosevelt*, 269, 270.
135. Ellison, *Theodore Roosevelt and Tales*, 8, 9; Austin Artz, as a history student at the University of North Dakota, did research built off Douglas Ellison's work on the claim by Hagedorn that Roosevelt asked to join the Stranglers in June 1884. Artz's paper "Eris of the West" refutes this claim and explains how it came to be believed. You can download a copy of his award-winning paper by searching for Austin H. Artz History 440 Research Paper, The Eris of the West.
136. *Mineral Argus*, July 3, 1884.
137. Barrows, *U-Bet*, 203.
138. Mueller, "Central Montana Vigilante Raids," 23.

139. Tye, *Some Things About the Vigilante Raid.*
140. Abbott, Smith and Tyler, *We Pointed Them North*, 108, 109.
141. Mueller, "Central Montana Vigilante Raids," 26.
142. Ibid., 28.
143. The region where these camps were located is now within the UL Bend and Charles M. Russell National Wildlife Refuges, just as wild today as it was in 1884. The camp locations were all inundated by the Fort Peck reservoir.
144. This, according to Otis Tye's account, who was quoting Billy Down's father, and confirmed by a person who claimed to be with the vigilantes that Tye met later.
145. *Sun River Sun*, August 28, 1884.
146. The names of old man James's sons are given in the *Sun River Sun*, August 28, 1884. And yes, Yam is a real name. This same newspaper claimed that Yam James and Dutchy Rolles were part of the gang that held up the military pay wagon.
147. Mueller, "Central Montana Vigilante Raids," 29.
148. *Sun River Sun*, August 28, 1884.
149. Here is the list of all those present at the James wood yard fight: Granville Stuart, Floppin Bill Cantrell, Jim Hibbs, Lynn Patterson, Bill Clark, Jack Ludvig, Charles Pettit, Butch Starley, John Single, J.L. Stuart, Andrew Fergus, Gus Adams, Jack Tabor and William Burnett.
150. Zogbaum, *Horse, Foot, and Dragoons*, 169.
151. Smith, *Champion Buffalo Hunter*, loc. 2107, Kindle; Taylor, *Kaleidoscopic Lives*, 91.
152. Tye, "Some Things About the Vigilantes."
153. Ibid.

Chapter 7

154. Mueller, "Central Montana Vigilante Raids," 35.
155. Ibid., 27.
156. Shafer, "Early History." George Shafer related the committee's work in the territory in the fall of 1884.
157. Stuart, *Forty Years on the Frontier*, 219.
158. *Mineral Argus*, January 22, 1885.
159. Should we call them vigilantes anymore since they are working as deputized stock inspectors? I would say yes because they had authority to

arrest, but they exceeded that authority and meted out justice as they saw fit, circumventing due process.

160. *Bad Lands Cowboy*, March 6, 1884. Montana stock inspector William Smith came to investigate this theft.
161. Ibid.
162. Burdick, *Life and Exploits*.
163. Shafer, "Early History."
164. *Sun River Times*, 1884.
165. Shafer, "Early History."
166. Berry, SHSND.
167. Stuart, *Forty Years on the Frontier*, 78.
168. Burdick, *Tales from Buffalo Land*, 95.
169. This is the range of numbers given by seven different sources. Goodall (delivered fifteen horses), Shafer (about twenty), Johnson's report in Burlington (sixteen), the Barton folk song (eighteen), Hackett at Souris City (sixteen), Bragg at their camp at the Slides (seventeen) and Billy Adams at Buford (seventeen); Burdick, *Tales from Buffalo Land*, 95. Baldwin claimed forty stayed at his ranch; *River Press*, October 22, 1884. This article claimed a posse of sixty crossed the Missouri; perhaps this was a mishearing of sixteen or exaggeration, which the newspapers of the day often did.
170. Burdick, *Tales from Buffalo Land*, 86.
171. Smith, *Champion Buffalo Hunter*, loc. 2114, Kindle.
172. Charlie Krug arrived early in Montana and worked for the railroad. He became a successful rancher and banker. He is said to be the first millionaire of Glendive, Montana.
173. Hyatt, *Uncommon Journey*, 179.
174. *Bad Lands Cowboy*, October 30, 1884.
175. Smith, *Champion Buffalo Hunter*, loc. 1983–4, Kindle.
176. Di Silvestro, *Theodore Roosevelt in the Bad Lands*, 141.
177. Sewall, *Bill Sewall's Story of T.R.*, 24.
178. Ibid., 22, 23.
179. Shafer, "Early History."
180. *Bad Lands Cowboy*, October 1, 1885.
181. Ibid.
182. Sewall, *Bill Sewall's Story of T.R.*, 18.
183. University of Minnesota, "With a Bang: Not a Whimper." Archived from the original (PDF) on June 22, 2010. The winters of 1882–83 to 1887–88 are called the Little Ice Age of the 1880s. This cold snap started before Krakatoa but was made even worse by this eruption.

184. Mueller, "Central Montana Vigilante Raids," 33, 34.
185. Pierre Wibaux was from the French aristocracy like the marquis, but unlike so many others he was very successful. After the winter of 1886–87, he ended up as sort of a last man standing, buying out the remnants of other ranchers' herds.
186. Shafer, "Early History."
187. Ibid. Shafer's order of events is confusing; he would have them back tracking. I am recording each ranch in the order they come up the river.
188. Harry Roberts, *As I Remember* (a self-published book that is now out of print).
189. Ibid.
190. One source that corroborates the George Shafer account is an article in the *Bad Lands Cowboy* of Medora dated October 30, 1884.
191. Jap Holts and Frank Chase were friends, but during a drinking bout Chase had to kill Holts to save his own life in April 1888. *Dickenson Press*, April 28, 1888.
192. Shafer, "Early History."
193. *River Press*, October 22, 1884.
194. Burdick, "Ranches in the Great American Desert," 295–96.
195. *Bad Lands Cowboy*, November 20, 1884.
196. Buffalo is mentioned in the Otis Tye account. He was reported to be at Grinnell Landing in late summer.
197. This story is passed on by many sources. Some say Bronson was shot and Buffalo hanged.
198. Burdick, *Tales from Buffalo Land*, 153.
199. Where did the chair come from? Did they bring him over the river to the Baldwin Ranch, which was located at Nesson Flats? Maybe they took him into Fort Buford. Did the gang have a cabin on Tobacco Garden Creek where all of this transpired?
200. Shafer, "Early History."
201. Smith, *Champion Buffalo Hunter*, loc. 1022–4. Vic Smith tells of a friend, Red Mike, whose real name was Mike Welch. In 1885, he was murdered by a wolfer named Doyle after a quarrel. Yellowstone Kelly was friends with a Mike Welsh who lived in Carroll, Montana, in the 1870s.

Chapter 8

202. Wick, *North Dakota Place Names*, 69.

203. *Bismarck Tribune*, November 16, 1884.
204. Burdick, *Jim Johnson Pioneer*, 27.
205. *Devil's Lake Inter-Ocean*, November 22, 1884. This article reports Simpson's death along with that of Francis Gardipee, although not captured at the same time or place. It is most likely the information about Simpson was given to Hackett by the Stranglers when they stayed at his house on November 7.
206. Burdick, *Tales From Buffalo Land*, 86.
207. This date is uncertain. We have a problem with the story. According to the *Devil's Lake Inter-Ocean*, November 22, 1884, the vigilantes were at Hackett's "one week ago last Friday." This would be November 7. However, Gardipee is in the custody of the Stranglers when they visit Burlington and in chains at the Berry Ranch afterward. They captured Gardipee first.
208. *Bismarck Weekly Tribune*, November 24, 1884.
209. Brown, *McHenry County*, 473.
210. *Burlington Centennial*, 23.
211. Ibid.
212. John Inkster, February 1, 1938, MSS10147, Box 006, John C. Eaton Papers, 1908 to 1958, SHSND [hereafter Inkster, SHSND].
213. Burill and Sitter, "Buffalo Bones on the Prairie," 19. From a 1928 interview with JB Rosencranz. Rosencranz said he lived next to one of this gang many years later (I think near Williston) and recognized him as having been one of the cowboys. Rosencranz asked him about the incident frequently, but the man would not talk about the subject.
214. Inkster, SHSND.
215. Brown, *McHenry County*, 21.
216. Burdick, *Jim Johnson Pioneer*, 28.
217. Berg, *Buffalo Wallows and Bayous*, 12. Some of the other things Clouse tells us about the vigilantes and horse thieves are incorrect.
218. *Burlington Centennial*, 58.
219. Berry, SHSND.
220. Mrs. Berry said Ravenwood was the big man, but this was recollected fifty-three years later. A better source suggests Bates had the size 12 boots, so more likely the big man. Ravenwood was a Métis; the description of a smaller wiry man would more likely be him.
221. *Bismarck Weekly Tribune*, March 1883. Ed Hackett tells of hearing a longtime resident of the area call himself the "Terror of This Mountain," meaning Dogden Mountain. This could have been Gardipee. Another likely candidate is Yankee Robinson.

222. *Bismarck Weekly Tribune*, November 24, 1884.
223. *Burlington Centennial*, 23.
224. Burdick, *Jim Johnson Pioneer*, 30.
225. Brown, *McHenry County*. Two skeletons turned up on the Rosencranz ranch along Mouse River while grading work was being done on the railroad.
226. Ibid., 21.
227. Ibid.
228. *Bismarck Weekly Tribune*, November 24, 1884, 8.
229. Brown, *McHenry County*, 21.
230. Ibid.
231. Observers in Burlington said all the cowboys were carrying rifles. I assume the Winchester Model 1873, as it was so common. The sketch by Zogbaum in chapter 6 shows how the rifle rested across the saddle at the ready.
232. *Washburn Times*, May 15, 1886. An unfolding story with many inaccuracies in this article.
233. Williams, *Pioneer Days of Washburn North Dakota*, 54.
234. *Burlington Centennial*, 23.
235. *Bismarck Weekly Tribune*, December 12, 1884.
236. *History of Mercer County*, 27.
237. *Bad Lands Cowboy*, November 4, 1884.
238. *Bismarck Weekly Tribune*, December 12, 1884.
239. *History of Mercer County*, 43, 44.
240. *Sun River Sun*, October 16, 1884.
241. *Fort Benton River Press*, September 22, 1886.
242. *Bismarck Weekly Tribune*, December 12, 1884.
243. Ibid.
244. Burdick, *Tales from Buffalo Land*, 167.
245. Ibid., 151.

Chapter 9

246. *Pioneers and Progress*, 48.
247. Brown, *McHenry County*, 22.
248. *Washburn Times*, December 19, 1884. Gives expression to the negative feelings toward Hackett.
249. *Bismarck Tribune*, December 19, 1885.

250. Ibid.
251. Ibid.
252. *Pioneers and Progress*, 48.
253. *Devil's Lake Inter-Ocean*, February 15, 1885.
254. Image borrowed from C.S. Lewis.
255. *Pioneers and Progress*, 48.
256. U.S. Census of 1870, St. Joseph, Pembina Territory.
257. *Devil's Lake Inter-Ocean*, March 28, 1885.
258. Ibid., March 21, 1885.
259. *Kalispell Bee*, October 10, 1905.
260. Ibid., June 10, 1902.
261. Ibid., October 10, 1905.
262. Certificate of Death, Flathead County, Mont. No. 786, Filed 24th Oct. 1905.
263. Barkwell, "Battle River Métis Scrip Applications," 9, 10. I cannot be sure these are the same people. This is the best match I could find in the genealogical records.
264. Williams, *Pioneer Days of Washburn North Dakota*, 54.
265. Lawrence Barkwell and Larry Haag, a PowerPoint pictorial essay on the Métis and Chippewa-Cree of the Pembina and Turtle Mountain areas.
266. Hayter, "Racially 'Indian,' Legally 'White.'"
267. McCord, *Calling the Brands*, 60–63.
268. From email correspondence with Joby Morey, great-great-great-grandson of Bill Cantrell. This is a family story passed on by his great-aunt Ellen.
269. *St. Joseph Gazette Herald*, September 27, 1900.

Epilogue

270. In the sweep of human history, the real mystery is not why there are periods of murder and killing. The real mystery comes when the killing stops. A better question is, Why did homicide disappear from Dakota? Why is it returning in recent years?

BIBLIOGRAPHY

Unpublished Materials

Artz, Austin. "The Eris of the West: The Origin and Genealogy of a Fabricated Narrative and How It Contaminated a Century of Theodore Roosevelt Historiography." Merrifield Competition Collection Series 25: 2018 Box 1, Orrin G. Libby Library, University of North Dakota.

Berry, Mrs. Tom. January 9th, 1937, MSS10147, Box 006, John C. Eaton Papers, 1908 to 1958, State Historical Society of North Dakota [SHSND].

Burill, Adah, and Eunice Sitter. "Buffalo Bones on the Prairie: A History of Towner, ND, 1865 to 1970." Master's thesis, University of North Dakota. August 1970.

The Burlington Centennial 1883–1983. Burlington, North Dakota.

Fort Buford Post Report Record of Events December 4th, 1883. SHSND.

Harvey, Mark. Fort Buford Research Files, 2000 MSS 11108 Box 1 SHSND.

History of Mercer County North Dakota, Commemorative of the 50th Anniversary of the First White Settlers, 1882 to 1932, SHSND.

Inkster, John. February 1st, 1938, MSS10147, Box 006, John C. Eaton Papers, 1908 to 1958, SHSND.

Pendroy, John MSS10147, Box 006, John C. Eaton Papers, 1908 to 1958, SHSND.

Robinson, Dr. John W. Tape #4 573A & B, at 1:27:50 State Historical Society North Dakota.

Staley, Charles T. (1863–1942). 1458. 20111 Manuscript, 1934. OCLC 17998480. Horse stealing; McLean County, North Dakota. SHSND.
Tye, Otis A. "Some Things About the Vigilantes Raid on The Upper Missouri in 1884 That Are Not Generally Known," 1560. 200036 SHSND
Watne, Ludwig. State Agency Record Historical Data Project Pioneer Biography #30529 SHSND.

Published Materials

Dakota Territorial Census of 1885, SHSND.
Montana County Births and Deaths, 1830–2011.
U.S. Census Records. 1850, Pembina County, Minnesota Territory.
———. 1850, McMinn County, Tennessee.
———. 1850, Bradley, Tennessee.
———. 1860, Between Red River and Big Stone River.
———. 1860, Hardin Conway Arkansas.
———. 1870, Pembina County Dakota Territory.

Articles

Barkwell, Lawrence. "Battle River Metis Scrip Applications." Academia.edu, 2022.
———. "Dakota-Métis Battle on the Grand Coteau:1851." Academia.edu.
———. "The Nehiyaw Pwat (Iron Alliance) Encounters with the Dakota." Academia.edu, 2019.
Barkwell, Lawrence, and Larry Haag. "A Power Point Pictorial Essay on the Métis and Chippewa-Cree of the Pembina and Turtle Mountain Areas." Academia.edu.
Bluemle, John P. "Gold in North Dakota." North Dakota State Government. https://www.dmr.nd.gov.
Burdick, Usher L. "Ranches in the Great American Desert." *North Dakota Historical Quarterly* 8, no. 4 (1941): 295–96.
Eriksmoen, Curt. "Friends Help Hackett Become Bismarck's First Mayor." *Bismarck Tribune*, April 10, 2016
Gordon, Greg. "Steamboats, Wood Hawks and War on the Upper Missouri River." *Montana: The Magazine of Western History*, 2011.

Hayter, Jennifer. "Racially 'Indian,' Legally 'White': The Canadian State's Struggles to Categorize the Métis, 1850–1900." Thesis, Department of History University of Toronto. Academia.edu.

Innis, Ben. "An Act of God." *Williston Herald*, 1976. Accessed February 12, 2022. http://georgegrinnell.blogspot.com.

Libby, O.G. Ed. *Collections of the State Historical Society of North Dakota*. Vol. 4. Fargo, ND: Knight Printing Co., 1913.

Lounsberry, Clement A. "Of the Burned Block at Bismarck." *The Record: Historical, Personal and Other Sketches, Politics, Literature and Education, Social and Fraternal Affairs, Illustrated* 4 (January 1898).

Mueller, Oscar O. "The Central Montana Vigilante Raids of 1884." *Montana Magazine of History*, 1951.

Paine, Phil. "The Hunters Who Owned Themselves." Academia.edu.

"Private Wilmot P. Sanford Diary." *North Dakota History* 33, no. 4 (Fall 1966): 335–78.

Shafer, George. "Early History of the Vigilantes." *Dickenson Press*, October 2, 1915.

St. Martin, Thomas. "With a Bang: Not a Whimper." Minnesota State Climatology Office. https://climateapps.dnr.state.mn.us.

Vyzralek, Frank E. "Murder in Masquerade: A Commentary on Lynching and Mob Violence in North Dakota's Past, 1882–1931." *North Dakota History: Journal of the Northern Plains* 57, no. 1 (Winter 1990): 20–29.

Newspapers

A North Dakota newspaper if state not given

Arkansas Democrat (Little Rock, AR)
Bad Lands Cowboy (Medora, DT)
Big Stone Herald
Bismarck Tribune
Bismarck Weekly Tribune
Burlington Republican
Cooperstown Courier
Daily Enterprise (Livingston, MT)
Devils Lake Inter-Ocean
Dickenson Press

Emmons County Record
Harrisburg (PA) Telegraph
Helena (MT) Weekly Herald
Jamestown Weekly Alert
Kalispell (MT) Bee
Mineral Argus (Maiden, MT)
River Press (Benton, MT)
St. Joseph (MO) Gazette Herald
Sun River Sun (Sun River, MT)
Washburn Times

Books

Abbott, Edward Charles, Helena Huntington Smith and Ronnie C. Tyler. *We Pointed Them North: Recollections of a Cowpuncher*. Norman: University of Oklahoma Press, 1955.

Barrows, John Rumsey. *U-Bet: A Greenhorn in Old Montana*. Lincoln: University of Nebraska Press, 1990.

Berg, M.L. *Buffalo Wallows and Bayous. A History of Minot, Dakota Territory 1886–1889*. Minot. ND: North American Heritage Press, 2008.

Bowers, Alfred. *Mandan Social and Ceremonial Organization*. Lincoln: University of Nebraska Press, 2004.

Breeling, Lutie Taylor. *When the Trail Was New in Mountraille*. Ross, ND: L.T. Breeling, 1956.

Brown, Corabella. *McHenry County: Its History and Its People*. Towner, ND: Mouse River Farmers Press, 1985.

Burdick, Usher L. *Jim Johnson Pioneer: A Brief History of the Mouse River Loop Country*. Courtesy of Digital Horizons (North Dakota Histories Collection, ND State Library) 1941.

———. *Life and Exploits of John Goodall. McKenzie County Farmer*. Watford City, ND, 1931.

———. *Tales from Buffalo Land: The Story of Fort Buford*. Baltimore: Wirth Brothers, 1940.

Chardon, Francis A. *Chardon's Journal at Fort Clark, 1834–1839*. Lincoln: University of Nebraska Press, 1997.

Custer, Elizabeth Bacon. *Following the Guidon*. London: Harper & Brothers, 1890.

Daschuk, James William. *Clearing the Plains: Disease, Politics of Starvation, and the Loss of Aboriginal Life*. Canada: University of Regina Press, 2013.

De Trobriand, Philippe Regis. *Military Life in Dakota: The Journal of Philip Regis De Trobriand*. Translated and Edited from the French original by Lucile M. Kane. Lincoln: University of Nebraska Press, 1982.

Dimsdale, Thomas Josiah, and Ruth Mather. *The Vigilantes of Montana*. Guilford, CT: Globe Pequot Press, 2003.

Di Silvestro, Roger L. *Theodore Roosevelt in the Badlands*. New York: Walker and Company, 2011.

Elderedge, D. *The Third New Hampshire and All About It*. Boston: EB Stillings and Company, 1893.

Ellison, Douglas W. *Theodore Roosevelt and Tales Told as Truth of His Time in the West.* Medora, ND: Western Edge Book Distributing, 2017.

Gourneau, Patrick. *History of the Turtle Mountain Band of Chippewa Indians*. Booklet published by the Turtle Mountain Band of Chippewa, 1980.

Hogue, Michel. *Métis and the Medicine Line: Creating a Border and Dividing a People*. Chapel Hill: University of North Carolina Press, 2015.

Hyatt, H. Norman. *An Uncommon Journey: The History of Old Dawson County, Montana Territory, the Biography of Stephen Norton Van Blaricom*. Helena, MT: Sweetgrass Books, 2009.

Kelly, Luther, and M.M. Quaife, ed. *Yellowstone Kelly: The Memoirs of Luther S. Kelly*. Lincoln: University of Nebraska Press, 1973.

McCord, Monty. *Calling the Brands: Stock Detectives in the Wild West.* United States: TwoDot, 2018.

Milner, Clyde A., II, and Carol A. O'Connor. *As Big as the West: The Pioneer Life of Granville Stuart*. New York: Oxford University Press, 2009.

Morris, Edmund. *The Rise of Theodore Roosevelt.* New York: Random House Trade Paperback, 1979.

Pfiefer, Michael J., ed. *The Roots of Rough Justice: Origins of American Lynching*. Urbana: University of Illinois Press, 2011.

Pioneers and Progress, Minnewaukan, North Dakota and Countryside. Minnewauken History Book Commission, 1983.

Roberts, Harry. *As I Remember.* (A self-published book that is now out of print), 1968.

Robinson, Elwyn B., *History of North Dakota*. Open Educational Resources. 1. https://commons.und.edu/oers/1, 2017.

Rodney, W. *Kootenai Brown His Life and Times*. 1st ed. Sydney, BC: Gray's Publishing, 1969.

Sewall, William Wingate. *Bill Sewall's Story of TR*. New York and London: Harper & Brothers, 1919.

Smith, Victor Grant. *The Champion Buffalo Hunter: The Frontier Memoirs of Yellowstone Vic Smith*. United States: TwoDot, 1997.

Stuart, Granville. *Forty Years on the Frontier*. Lincoln: University of Nebraska Press, 1977.

Taylor, Joseph Henry. *Kaleidoscopic Lives* (Abridged, Annotated). Big Byte Books. 1896. Kindle Edition, 2016.

———. *Sketches of Frontier and Indian Life on the Upper Missouri & Great Plains*. 1897. Kindle Edition, n.d.

Wick, Douglas A. *North Dakota Place Names*. Bismarck, ND: Hedemarken Collectibles, 1988.

Williams, Mary Ann Barnes. *Pioneer Days of Washburn North Dakota and Vicinity Books One and Two*. Originally published by the *Washburn Leader*. [North Dakota]: BHG Inc., 1995.

Zogbaum, Rufus Fairchild. *Horse, Foot, and Dragoons: Sketches of Army Life at Home and Abroad*. London: Harper & Brothers, 1888.

INDEX

M

N

W

Y

Z

ABOUT THE AUTHOR

Ron Berget grew up on a farm/ranch on the Crooked Lake mentioned in this book. He graduated from the University of North Dakota with a degree in Fish and Wildlife Management. Much to his surprise, he managed to get a job working for the U.S. Fish and Wildlife Service in Devils Lake, North Dakota, and later transferred to Hagerman National Wildlife Refuge in north Texas. He left the USFWS to attend and graduate from Dallas Theological Seminary.

Ron pastored churches in Minnesota for several decades and is currently Asia Director of a worldwide pastor training organization. This position has him traveling to many Asian countries each year.

His hobbies are bass fishing, hunting, wilderness trips and bird watching. In the long dark Minnesota nights, his hobby has been researching and writing on this book.

He has three married sons, ten grandchildren and a beautiful wife—all who encouraged him throughout the process. He currently resides sixty miles northwest of mythical Lake Wobegon, Minnesota. This is his first published book.

Ron N. Berget with Crooked Lake in background. *Photo by Eric Berget.*